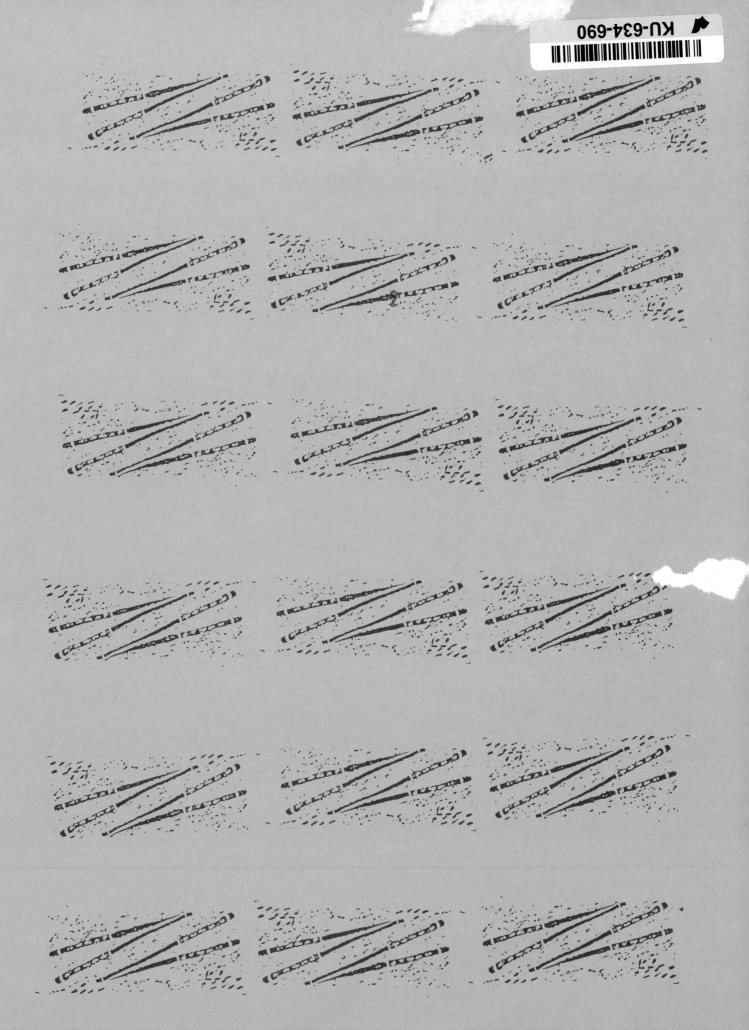

Spicy, fresh and stir-fried

Spicy, fresh and stir-fried

An exciting new look at the finest Oriental cooking

EDITED BY BEVERLEY LE BLANC

APPLE

A QUINTET BOOK

Published by The Apple Press
6 Blundell Street
London N7 9BH

ISBN 1-85076-683-5

This book was designed and produced by
Quintet Publishing Limited
6 Blundell Street
London N7 9BH

Creative Director: Richard Dewing
Designer: James Lawrence
Project Editor: Diana Steedman

The material in this publication previously
appeared in *The Great Chili Pepper Cookbook* by
Gina Steer, *Chinese Vegetarian Cooking* by
Deh-Ta Hsiung, *Fruit Fandango* by Moya
Clarke, *Step-by-Step Sushi* by Katsuji Yamamoto
and Roger W. Hicks, *Thai Cooking* by Kurt
Kahrs, *Vietnamese Cooking* by Paulette Do Van

Typeset in Great Britain by
Central Southern Typesetters, Eastbourne
Manufactured in China
by Regent Publishing Services Ltd
Printed in China
by Leefung-Asco Printers Ltd

CONTENTS

INTRODUCTION

Oriental cooking includes an exciting array of ingredients and flavours from China, Japan, Thailand, Vietnam and the other countries of Southeast Asia. To many Westerners, all foods from these distant lands may seem similar, but there is, in fact, great variety. Cooks in each of the countries place great emphasis on using fresh local ingredients, so rice and noodles are about the only staple ingredients used throughout the whole of the region.

CHINA

Not surprisingly, for such a vast country with a population of almost a billion and huge regional variations in climate and produce, Chinese cooking is diverse. These differences are reflected in the regional cooking styles. Yet, the fundamental character of Chinese cooking remains the same throughout the land: whether in the north (Peking cuisine) or in the south (Cantonese cooking), food is prepared and cooked in accordance with the same principles—most ingredients are cut up just before cooking with great emphasis on heat control and the harmonious blending of different flavours.

The chief distinguishing feature of Chinese cooking is that in the north, people rely primarily on wheat flour as a basic staple of their diet, while in the south, it is almost always rice. Some of the cooking methods may vary a little from region to region, and the emphasis on seasonings may differ, too, but they are all unmistakably Chinese.

Food from Szechwan in the west is hot and spicy, while Hunan food also features the sweet-and-sour flavour combinations with its spicy ingredients. Canton, in the south, is the home of many of the popular dishes on Western Chinese restaurant menus: egg rolls and fried rice.

The influence of Chinese cooks throughout the region is unmistakable. Stir-frying originating here, and this simple, quick technique is practised in most kitchens. The Chinese can also be credited with introducing soy sauce, made from fermented soybeans, to the region.

JAPAN

Perhaps more here than in any other country in the Orient, aesthetics play an important part in the preparation of food. Japanese cooks place great emphasis on freshness of ingredients and take great care in how they arrange food on serving platters. Many Japanese have a strong love of nature and this is often reflected in how food is presented.

Rice is the main staple of the Japanese diet and short-grain rice is served with almost every meal. Short-grain rice is also used a great deal in the preparation of sushi recipes (page 28).

THAILAND

Cooking in Thailand reflects the country's position at the crossroads of Southeast Asia, lying between two countries with great cuisines, India and China. It has also absorbed culinary traditions from other near neighbours, and as a result, the use of spices and variety are the two hallmarks of the country's cuisine. Taken all together, the influences from abroad—Indian flavours via Burma, Muslim dishes from Malaysia, sticky rice and rustic, bitter flavours from Laos and stir-fried wok cooking and steamed fish dishes from the Chinese immigrant population—have made Thai cooking so delicious.

The great regional variety of Thai cooking is often missing on Western restaurant menus, yet there are distinct culinary traditions. Naturally, it is the Gulf of Thailand that has supplied the country with many of its delicious seafood recipes, and the Central Plains region, where most of the country's rice is grown, is the heartland of traditional Thai cooking. Bangkok is the country's cultural melting pot, so its food has a Chinese flavour from the number of Chinese who live there, and it is also the home of the more refined royal cooking.

Thai curries often include coconut milk, and cooks add shrimp paste to many dishes as a standard flavouring. Other popular ingredients include peanuts, lemon grass, tamarind, coriander, and fiery-hot bird's-eye chillies.

VIETNAM

During Vietnam's history, it has been ruled by the Chinese and the French and it has had strong trading ties with Portugal and India, and each of these countries has contributed to Vietnam's cuisine.

From China the Vietnamese have adopted their love of noodles and the stir-frying method of cooking. The Vietnamese also borrowed soy sauce from the Chinese, and then went on to develop their own nuoc mam sauce (page 12). Made from fermented fish, this sauce accompanies most meals in a Vietnamese home. Its strong, pungent fish smell becomes much milder when combined with food and it adds a flavour that is distinctly Vietnamese.

Neighbouring Laos, Cambodia and Thailand have influenced the Vietnamese in their use of fresh herbs. No Vietnamese meal is complete without there being at least two or three fresh herbs present, either as a garnish or in their own right as part of the meal. The Vietnamese also love to wrap up their food in fresh lettuce leaves and to include one or two herbs; the favourites are coriander, mint, basil, dill and fennel.

The Indians and Portuguese brought spices and developed the combinations of ingredients that in the West have come to be known as curries. The French, who colonized Vietnam, forced the Vietnamese to be inventive—under the regime the peasants had to create wonderful dishes from the leftover pieces of animals that were not commandeered by their European masters. The Vietnamese have traditionally used caramel and glazes to create original tastes and to preserve ingredients, but from the French they also discovered coffee and French bread.

ORIENTAL INGREDIENTS

BAMBOO SHOOTS

are sold in tins and should be eaten as soon as possible after opening the tin. They will, however, last for up to 6 days in a refrigerator if the water in which they are stored is changed daily. Use these ivory-coloured shoots to add texture to stir-fries.

BANH PHO

are short, flat, white Vietnamese rice stick noodles about 2.5 mm (⅛ in) wide. They cook in minutes in boiling water or soup and should not be overdone. They are used in soup-noodle dishes, particularly the Hanoi soup that goes by the common name of *pho*.

BANH TRANG OR RICE PAPER

is the Vietnamese equivalent of ravioli skins. It is round, semi-transparent, thin, hard and dry rice paper and is used as the wrapping on Vietnamese egg rolls and grilled meats, with salad and herbs. It is made from a dough of finely ground rice, water and salt, with tapioca (cassava) flour as a binding agent.

The dough is passed through rollers and then cut into circles 18 to 35 cm (7 to 14 in) in diameter. These are then put on bamboo mats to dry in the sun. Once dry, they will keep indefinitely. To use, they must be moistened by covering with a damp cloth until soft or by dipping quickly into warm water. To get a crisp, golden-brown colour, the wrappers can be brushed lightly with a sugar-water solution before frying.

BEANSPROUTS

are widely available fresh. They can be kept in the refrigerator for 2 to 3 days. Tinned beansprouts should not be used as they do not have the crunchy texture which is the main characteristic of this popular vegetable.

BONITO

Small tuna, favoured by many Oriental chefs for their strong flavour. Diced bonito flakes, sold at Oriental grocery stores, flavour Japanese soups.

CELLOPHANE NOODLES

are noodles resembling strands of clear plastic and are also called transparent noodles or bean-thread noodles. Cooked as noodles, they are used in soups, braised dishes and hotpots. In Szechwan and neighbouring Tibet, they are first softened in water and then stir-fried with vegetables. In Indonesia, Malaysia and Singapore, the boiled noodles are added to sweet drinks and desserts together with palm sugar syrup, coconut milk and diced vegetables, such as yam or sweet potato, or sweet corn kernels.

CHILIES

exist in many variations, varying in size and shape as well as colour and intensity of flavour. Generally, green chillies are milder than the red ones, and seeding them reduces their intensity. Red or green bird's-eye chillies, from Thailand, are especially hot.

Whole, fresh chillies may be added directly to dishes or may be chopped and shredded into curries, soups and stir-fries, or mixed with soy sauce, vinegar, or fish sauce to be used as dips. They may be dried or steeped in oil to make a clear, hot-flavoured oil, which is used extensively in China.

CHILI BEAN PASTE

is fermented bean paste mixed with salt, flour and a hot chilli. It is sold in jars. If you don't have any, combine chilli paste with yellow bean sauce.

CHINESE MUSHROOMS

is the common name for the dried black (or rather pale buff or brown) mushrooms. The best are lighter coloured with plump caps, but they are very expensive. Long ago the Chinese learned that drying the mushrooms intensifies their flavour.

They should be soaked in warm water for about 30 minutes, then squeezed to get rid of the salt. The stems should be cut off because they are too tough to eat. The caps are particularly good when they are simmered gently in a light broth with soy sauce and rice wine.

Selection of mushrooms in Oriental cooking:

WOOD EAR MUSHROOMS
FRESH BLACK MUSHROOMS
FRESH OYSTER MUSHROOMS
TINNED STRAW MUSHROOMS
DRIED CHINESE MUSHROOMS

FRESH BUTTON MUSHROOMS
TINNED OYSTER MUSHROOMS
WOOD EAR MUSHROOMS
TINNED ABALONE MUSHROOMS
TINNED CHINESE MUSHROOMS

CORIANDER LEAVES

are used extensively in Southeast Asian cooking, although they are hardly used in Japan. The flavour is fresh, strong, earthy and something of an acquired taste. Also called Chinese parsley or fresh coriander.

CORIANDER ROOTS

are used particularly in Thailand, where they are ground together with the stems to make curry pastes and sauces. There the leaves are used in salads and as a garnish.

COCONUT MILK

was originally made by painstakingly grating the kernel and mixing it with a little water. The resulting mixture then had to be squeezed through a piece of cloth. Today with the advent of the food processor, the kernel is ground together with a little water and the mixture squeezed by hand, a much faster process. The first squeeze produces the best milk and is called coconut cream (do not confuse this with cream of coconut). After a second squeeze, the dry fibre pulp is thrown away. There are a number of excellent brands of tinned coconut milk available, but it should be remembered that it will keep for only a few hours at room temperature, or 2 days in a refrigerator. If there is a great deal left over, it should be frozen.

A third way of making coconut milk is to soak desiccated coconut in hot water or milk and squeeze this through a piece of cloth in the traditional manner. The first squeeze is very rich and tends to curdle during cooking. To avoid this, continual stirring is recommended. Cream of coconut is sold in bar form at Oriental and Asian grocery stores. It is dissolved in boiling water to make a slightly thickened, creamy liquid.

CUMIN

is Mediterranean in origin and has travelled east. It is both pungent and aromatic. The seeds should be roasted in a dry pan or in a very hot oven before using, either whole or ground. The temperature should be high enough to make them pop.

DRIED JELLYFISH

has little taste but is valued for its crunchy texture. It is the salted and sun-dried skin of the mantle of the jellyfish and said by Westerners to be as tasty as a rubber band. It should be soaked in warm water for several hours and does not require cooking, which only serves to toughen it. It is usually shredded finely and marinated in vinegar to be served in a salad. Add a little sesame oil and it is transformed into the most delicious and crunchy salad.

FIVE-SPICE POWDER

is an aromatic, Chinese spice powder, made according to an ancient formula using three native spices—star anise, cassia bark and Szechwan peppercorns—with the seeds of wild fennel and cloves from the nearby Moluccas or Spice Islands.

The five spices in their whole form can be used as an Oriental bouquet garni, tied up in a small muslin bag and put into stews and the like and retrieved before serving. Five-spice powder can also be made into a dip by adding five-spice powder to heated salt.

You can make your own five-spice powder by placing 40 Szechwan peppercorns; 2 cinnamon sticks, 2 inches long; 7.5 ml (1½ teaspoons) fennel seeds; 12 whole cloves; and 2 whole star anise in a mortar or spice grinder and grind to a fine powder. This should produce about 30 ml (2 tbsp) five-spice powder. Store in a tightly closed jar. It will keep for about three months.

To make five-spice salt, heat a wok or pan over medium heat. Pour in 60 ml (4 tbsp) salt and heat through, stirring continuously, until well heated. Cool briefly before stirring in the five-spice powder. When cool, the mixture can be stored in a spice jar. It can be used as a dip for roasted, grilled or broiled and fried meats, or sprinkled over food as a seasoning prior to deep-frying.

GALANGAL

(greater and lesser species) is a member of the ginger family and, in many countries, is used as a substitute for ginger. It has a hot, peppery taste and is used mainly as a flavouring. In Thailand, greater galangal is ground along with chillies and other herbs as well as spices, to make a refreshing drink.

Lesser galangal is often eaten as a vegetable, both raw and cooked. However, in Indonesia, lesser galangal is used as a spice.

GINGER

is one of the basic ingredients of Oriental cooking. A knobbly root, fresh root ginger should be peeled if it is to be sliced or chopped, but it can be left unpeeled if it is to be grated on an Oriental grater. It has a hot, peppery flavour.

When preserved in vinegar, it is often included in rustic recipes or used as a garnish. It is considered a delicacy in Japan.

GLUTEN

A high-gluten flour and water dough is soaked and kneaded in water to wash out the starch, and the remaining gluten is porous like a sponge. This is cut into pieces to be used like dumplings to carry flavour and provide bulk in sauces. Buy gluten in Oriental supermarkets.

GROUND CHILLIES

are made from dried pods, which are also used whole, broken or shredded. They are best dried by roasting in a hot oven or in a dry pan. They are then ground to a coarse powder which is then added to ground rice. This mixture is used as a strongly flavoured thickener or coating for fried foods. It may also be sprinkled over foods as a condiment.

GROUND CORIANDER

is one of the essential ingredients in curry powders. It is made from the seed spice and it is best to buy the seed spice whole and grind it when needed. To get the best out of the coriander seed, it is advisable to toast first in an oven and then grind it finely.

HOISIN SAUCE

is the barbecue sauce of Southeast Asia. Made from red rice which is coloured with a natural food dye, usually annatto seeds, it is a sweet-tasting, thick, reddish-brown sauce best used as a condiment for roast pork and poultry.

It is made from fermented soybean paste, sugar, garlic and spices, normally five-spice powder. Hoisin sauce should not be confused with the Chinese barbecue sauce, *sha cha jiang*.

LEMON GRASS

has been used in Southeast Asia and in Europe for centuries under the better-known name *citronella*, named for its distinct lemon scent and flavor. It is best used fresh, but can be kept, loosely wrapped, in the refrigerator for about 10 days. To store, the bulb end should be rinsed and dried, then finely sliced or chopped. When ready for use, it should be slit open lengthwise to release the flavour.

LOTUS ROOTS

are the rose-coloured roots of an aquatic plant. It is sold tinned and fresh or dried in Oriental grocery stores. Use it in both sweet and savoury dishes.

MIRIN

also called rice wine, is used in Japanese cooking, including the preparation of sushi, to add sweetness.

NOODLES

are one of the mainstays in the Oriental diet and were the inspiration for spaghetti. They are used extensively in Vietnam where they are enjoyed, in some form, at every meal.

Dried noodles should be kept in an airtight container where they will last for several months. They are usually cooked by boiling in salted water, like pasta.

NORI

are paper-thin sheets of seaweed used to make sushi. They will range in colour from black to deep green. Buy nori in Japanese supermarkets.

NUOC MAM

sauce is a powerfully flavoured, pungent seasoning sauce. It is used extensively in Southeast Asia, particularly Burma, Cambodia, Thailand and Vietnam. It is made by layering fish and salt into large barrels and allowing the fish to ferment for at least 3 months before the accumulated liquid is siphoned off, filtered and bottled.

In Vietnam nuoc mam is made into different dipping sauces by adding chillies, ground, roasted peanuts, sugar and other ingredients. It is very much an acquired taste, and substitutes such as soy sauce are sufficiently exotic.

OYSTER SAUCE

is one of the most popular bottled sauces in Southeast Asia. Made from dried oysters, it is thick and richly flavoured. The cheaper brands tend to be salty. The original sauce was much thinner and contained fragments of fermented, dried oysters. Many people use it as a superior version of soy sauce, but Asians use it as an accompaniment for stir-fried vegetables and to flavour and colour braised and stir-fried dishes.

PAPRIKA

is also known as capsicum or peppers. In Vietnam it is used as a vegetable and as a spice. In its latter guise, it is dried and ground to a powder.

POMELO

is a large Chinese fruit that resembles a grapefruit. It tapers slightly at the stem end and has a thick, sweet, slightly rough-textured skin and a dry, semisweet flesh. Like many other fruits, it is sometimes eaten in Southeast Asia with salt.

RED BEAN PASTE

This reddish-brown paste is made from blended red beans and crystal sugar. It is sold in tins and, once opened, the contents should be transferred to a covered container and kept in the refrigerator (it keeps for several months). Sweetened blended chestnuts can be substituted.

SALTED BLACK BEANS

Very salty indeed! Sold in plastic bags, jars or tins. Should be crushed with water or rice wine before use. They will keep indefinitely in a covered jar.

RICE VERMICELLI

is a fine, extruded, creamy-coloured noodle, made from a dough of finely ground rice and water. It cooks almost instantly, needing only to be dipped in very hot water and drained thoroughly.

Rice vermicelli can be stir-fried and served as soft noodles. It should be softened first and drained before stir-frying. To deep-fry, the dried noodles are added directly to the oil.

SALTED COD

was first imported from Newfoundland in Canada as survival food for the natives of British colonies. Just how it found its way to Vietnam is not clear but it has become something of a delicacy of not only Southeast Asia but the West Indies and Africa as well. It can be bought in most ethnic food stores.

SESAME OIL

Sold in bottles and widely used in China as a garnish rather than for cooking. The refined yellow sesame oil sold in Middle Eastern stores is not as aromatic, has less flavour and is, therefore, not a very satisfactory substitute. Sesame oil is usually added at the end of cooking so its delicate flavour and aroma are not destroyed by the heat.

SAKE

is made by introducing a yeast mould into steamed rice to begin the fermentation process. Later lactic acid is added to prevent contamination. The milky fermentation is then filtered and, about 45 days later, results in a crystal clear liquid—sake.

The word itself is the name for Japan's most popular beverage and all Japanese alcoholic drinks. Connoisseurs advise that it be drunk immediately and, once the bottle is opened, it should be finished the same day. In any event, sake should not be left undrunk for more than a year.

SOY SAUCE

is made from fermented soybeans mixed with a roasted grain, normally wheat. It is injected with a yeast mould and after fermentation begins, salt is added. Yeast is added for further fermentation and the liquid is left in vats for several months and then filtered.

Light soy sauce is thin, salty and light in flavour, and is used as a condiment and in cooking where its light colour will not spoil the colours of the ingredients, particularly seafood.

Dark soy sauce is thicker with a full-bodied flavour and is used to add colour where needed. Generally it is less salty than the light soy sauce. The Chinese mushroom soy sauce is made with the addition of flavourings from Chinese straw mushrooms.

Lu Soy is a "master sauce" made from soy sauce with sugar, ginger and five-spice, and is used for simmering poultry and other meats that benefit from a rich flavour and a dark colour.

Sweet soy sauce is a dark, sweet sauce made with soy sauce, sugar and malt sugar. It has a distinctive malty taste, which makes it ideal as a dip for fried snacks, poultry and seafood.

STRAW MUSHROOMS

are grown on paddy-straw, left over from harvested wheat, which gives them a distinctly earthy taste. Generally, they are packed in water and tinned. They are globe-shaped, about the size of quail eggs, and buff-coloured, growing grey-black as they become older. They have no stems but a cross section reveals an internal stem.

SZECHWAN PEPPERCORNS

are aromatic, small, red-brown seeds from the prickly ash tree known as fagara. The whole "peppercorns" can be kept for years without loss of flavour if stored in a tightly sealed jar away from light, heat and moisture. In China, they are mixed into heated fine salt to produce pepper-salt, a fragrant, salty dip for grilled and fried foods, and often used in marinades.

SZECHWAN PRESERVED VEGETABLES

is a specialty of Szechwan. It is the root of a special variety of green mustard pickled in salt and chilli. It is sold in tins, and once opened, should be stored in a tightly covered container; it will keep for months in the refrigerator.

STAR ANISE

is the seed pods of one of the Magnolia trees. The tan-coloured, eight-pointed pods resemble stars, hence the name. When dried, a shiny, flat, light brown seed is revealed in each point. It has a pronounced licorice flavour and the ground spice is one of the essential ingredients in the Chinese five-spice powder. In Vietnam it is used primarily in simmered dishes and for making stock.

SUGAR CANE

is reasonably easy to obtain from large grocers, West Indian shops and some markets that specialize in foreign produce. It is cultivated exclusively for its sweet sap that is made into sugar.

The sugar cane bought for cooking consists of the stem, the leaves being chopped off in the cane fields. The cane should be very carefully peeled with a strong, sharp knife.

TIGER LILY BUDS

Known as "yellow flower" or "golden needles" in Chinese, these are dried buds, golden yellow in colour. They have to be soaked and rinsed in water before use. Will keep indefinitely.

TOFU

also called bean curd, is made from dried soybeans, soaked, puréed, and boiled with water. The resulting milky liquid is strained and then mixed with a coagulant or natural solidifier which causes it to form curds. These are then taken to wooden tubs lined with cloth and pressed until they form bean curd.

The tofu is then cut into small squares and stored in cold water. Fresh bean curd is inexpensive and easily available. Although it is bland, it absorbs the flavours in which it is cooked. It was discovered during the Han Dynasty by a group of researchers who were assigned to investigate new medicines. Their result was bean curd, which became known as "meat without bones." Dried tofu skins are sold in Oriental grocery stores.

TURMERIC

a native of Southeast Asia, belonging to the same family as ginger and galangal. It has a bright orange-yellow flesh with a strong, earthy smell and a slightly bitter taste. The flesh is responsible for the yellow colour we associate with curry powders and turmeric overpowers all other spices.

Dried turmeric is best stored in a tightly sealed jar, kept in a dark place and used with discretion. Like many spices in the East, it is credited with medicinal qualities and for this can be taken both internally and externally.

WASABI

often called Japanese horseradish, is a green paste made from a root that has a sharp, pungent flavour. It is sold as a paste or a powder, which should be mixed with water. Wasabi is traditionally served with sushi.

WATER CHESTNUTS

Available in tins only. Once opened, they will keep in fresh water for 2 to 3 weeks in a covered jar in the refrigerator.

WOOD EAR FUNGUS

is known under a variety of names. Perhaps the most common is derived from its habitat of decayed wood. The Chinese call it cloud ears because it resembles the clouds rendered with a paint brush in a Chinese painting. It is also called Judas or Jew's ear from its botanical name (*Auricularia auriculajudae*) or perhaps some other inspiration, and the Thai translation is rat's ear.

It is valued for its subtle, delicate flavour and slightly crunchy "bite." It is always sold in its dried form and looks like a curly seaweed. When soaked, it expands to 5 times its dried size, so a little goes a long way. It should be rinsed thoroughly to wash out the grains of sand that seem to cling to it. It does not require long cooking and does not have any flavour of its own but readily absorbs seasonings. It does not like moisture and should be stored in a sealed container in a cool, dry place.

YELLOW BEAN SAUCE

is made according to the ancient recipe for jiang or pickled yellow soybeans in a salty liquid. It is normally bought in tins but it is best transferred to a jar in which it can be stored in a refrigerator almost indefinitely.

ORIENTAL
KITCHEN EQUIPMENT

When cooking Oriental food, there are a few kitchen utensils that you are certain to find useful. They are not absolutely essential—Oriental food can be cooked using perfectly regular Western utensils—but they do make life easier.

WOK

The first thing you are going to need is a wok. This is a thin, curved pan traditionally used in the East, particularly by the Chinese. It is now coming into its own around the world.

The first woks were beaten out of tempered steel to make use of heat efficiently and quickly—they originated in China, where wood and fuel are at a premium. To make them even more efficient, they were curved to fit snugly over the flames of the Chinese brazier. To the Chinese and other people living in the East, the wok is the complete cooking utensil, used for frying, stir-frying, deep-frying, boiling, braising and steaming.

Woks come in different sizes and are made with different materials. For the average Western home, the ideal size is the 35-cm (14-in) wok. It is available in carbon, tempered or stainless steel, and with a nonstick coating. The really hi-tech cook may even have a plug-in electrical wok made of carbon steel, possibly with a nonstick coating.

Woks are generally available in the larger stores in kit form, which includes a stand, lid, steaming rack and a multitude of small accessories. You should be careful to get a good, well-fitting lid, preferably not made of carbon or tempered steel as these are heavy and can rust—much better is the cheaper aluminum lid, or a stainless steel one.

Some woks have a pair of handles, normally of the same material as the wok; others have just the one wooden handle. If you have a strong wrist the single-handled wok is probably better, but if you are the least bit apprehensive about lifting and tossing around a heavy pan, you might be better off with the double-handled wok.

Carbon or tempered steel woks are traditional. Although they are made of thin metal they are quite heavy, and, without care, rust very easily. To prevent this you need to rub them lightly with some oiled absorbent kitchen paper and keep them in a dry place. They come with a wax coating which is easily removed by a brisk rub in hot soapy water. The wok should be rinsed and dried, then put on a very high flame and allowed to smoke. Pour in a little oil and rub it around the pan, making sure you include the rim as well. Do this a couple of times and then wipe the outside with oiled absorbent kitchen paper and leave to cool. Your wok will now be "seasoned."

Oriental chefs rarely wash their woks, so simply wipe yours with absorbent kitchen paper. If you feel the need for scouring, then do it with some salt. When you are satisfied that the surface is acceptably clean, wipe with oiled absorbent kitchen paper. If you wash your wok with soap, you should re-season it as above.

The stainless steel wok does not have a rust problem and is easier to clean, but it does have a couple of disadvantages: it is not easily obtainable and it is not as responsive to heat as the traditional wok. However, some are slightly flattened on the bottom and, therefore, more suitable for using on electric cookers, and you can use soap and water as often as you want without having to re-season. (If you want to use a regular wok on an electric cooker you can buy a ring on which it will sit.)

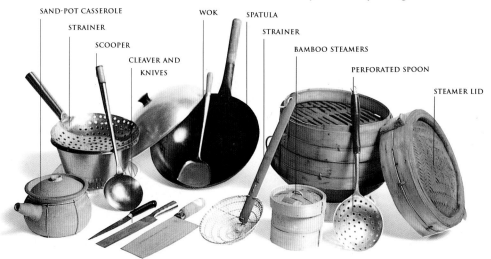

SAND-POT CASSEROLE
STRAINER
SCOOPER
CLEAVER AND KNIVES
WOK
SPATULA
STRAINER
BAMBOO STEAMERS
PERFORATED SPOON
STEAMER LID

The nonstick wok does not need seasoning, nor is it affected by soap. However, as with most nonstick pans, metal utensils and metal pot scourers should not be used. Once the nonstick surface has been scratched it is practically useless, and the utensil reverts to being a traditional wok.

The electric wok is the latest and most hi-tech of the woks. Most have a nonstick surface. It is virtually a portable kitchen, being a combination of cooker and saucepan, and can also be used as a serving dish.

WOK ACCESSORIES

A double wooden-handled wok with wok brush, and a single-handled wok on a wok stand with long-handled metal strainer, and a smaller perforated ladle.

If you buy your wok at a specialist store instead of at a regular food store where kits are *de rigueur*, you might consider buying a few accessories at the same time.

To keep the wok steady on a modern stovetop, you will probably need a wok stand. This is particularly useful if you are steaming or deep-frying but it can be dispensed with when stir-frying since everything is happening so quickly and sudden changes of temperature are essential.

A wok brush is a very useful piece of equipment to have in your kitchen. Made from wood or bamboo, it is used to clean the wok after use. The stiffness of the brush works in much the same way as a scourer, except that it does not scratch the coating produced by seasoning the wok.

Bamboo steamers are equally useful (buy wood trivets at the same time). The advantage of having bamboo steamers is that they can be stacked one on top of the other and several dishes can be cooked at the same time. They are particularly good for warming up leftovers.

A bamboo strainer, made of a reinforced circle of wire netting with a wooden handle, is handy for lifting ingredients from steam or hot oil, and a wok scoop to toss and turn ingredients when stir-frying seems to work much better than a Western ladle.

You might also like to buy a cleaver. They have wooden handles and come in three weights: light, medium, and heavy. They are made of either tempered carbon steel or stainless steel. The former is preferable since it is harder and maintains a sharper cutting edge for a longer time. For most Oriental cooking it is a case of the sharper the better. Contrary to what people tend to believe, sharper knives are much safer than dull ones, which slip and slide and demand much more effort.

USING A CLEAVER

Before you put your kitchen to work, you should know two more things. The first is how to sharpen your cleaver. You will need a small abrasive stone with a rough and a smooth honing surface. The rough is used for dull and nicked edges while the smooth is used for keeping good cleavers in perfect condition.

Begin by rinsing and drying the cleaver, then sprinkle a few drops of oil or water on the rough side of the stone. Hold the cleaver with the sharp edge away from you and the blade almost flat, then rub it on the stone by pressing the fingers of the left hand (for right-handed people) lightly on the top surface. Rub it back and forth several times without lifting it, then turn it over and repeat. Rinse the cleaver to remove any stray metal particles, then rub it on the smooth surface of the stone a few times to polish the blade.

The second thing you need to know is how to hold the cleaver. There are three ways to do this and each serves a different function. To chop, you need to curl your fingers around the handle with your thumb on the side of the blade. Chop with decisive strokes, using your entire arm and not just your wrist. Firm, decisive chopping means no splintering of bones.

To mince meat, a common technique in Oriental cooking, you need to hold the cleaver with your fingers and thumb curled around the handle. The tip of the cutting edge is used as a fulcrum and the blade lifted and dropped, the weight of the cleaver doing all the work. Mincing is very quick; it is even quicker if you use two cleavers, working them up and down alternately, but this requires some practice.

Finally, the cutting grip. Hold the cleaver as for chopping but instead of curling your index finger around the handle, press it against the blade. With your thumb pressing on the other side of the blade, you have maximum control. This way, you can tilt and turn the blade every which way. In most Oriental cooking, all food is cut into uniformly small pieces. The reason for this is simple: small pieces cook quickly without losing their crunchiness, and if they are the same size they will be uniformly crunchy. It also means that they absorb the taste of the oil and seasonings much more efficiently in spite of the short cooking time.

Cleavers can be used for chopping practically everything once you know the technique. To use the cleaver, grasp the handle firmly with your index finger resting on one side of the blade and your thumb pressing against that finger on the other side.

Most Oriental cooking insists on ingredients retaining their natural shape—for example, cauliflower and broccoli are cut into flowerets. Other vegetables are sliced, shredded, diced or roll cut, depending on the method of cooking. For stir-frying, vegetables are cut as thinly as possible, even shredded, while for braising they are cut into larger pieces. The theory behind this advanced culinary technology is that you have much more surface to be exposed to a quick blast of heat for the one type of cooking and less surface for longer cooking, thereby sealing in and retaining the flavours.

Oriental chefs use cuts that are different from what you may be accustomed to, but there is a perfectly rational explanation. For instance, to chop poultry, you disjoint the wings first. There is a trick to doing it briskly and effectively: there always is. Snap them back, expose the connecting bone and cut through. The same goes for the legs and thighs. Wings are normally chopped crosswise into three pieces, while a leg and thigh would be chopped into five, leaving the major joints—where the upper wing meets the lower and the thigh meets the drumstick—intact. Part of the reason for this is that Orientals are fond of the crunchy cartilage found there. A second advantage is that reassembly is much easier and the finished product looks a lot better.

The bird is then put on its side and with one or more judicious whacks the backbone and breast are separated. The breast is then placed bones down, chopped lengthwise and separated. Each half is then cut crosswise in three pieces. The back is cut in a similar fashion. To reassemble, follow the exactly opposite procedure—in other words, lay down the backbone first, then the breast and finally the thighs, drumsticks and wings.

Oriental cooks also use the cleaver for mincing meat, and once you get accustomed to it, you too will come to the inescapable conclusion that there is a difference in taste between meat that goes through a machine and that which you do yourself.

To mince meat, poultry or seafood, cut them into coarse pieces and then pile the pieces up. Mince by using the tip of the wet cleaver as a fulcrum and saw away; alternatively, chop firmly and swiftly down using a short action. Chop from one end of the pile to the other, then chop again, this time at an angle of 90°. Repeat this several times, then slip the cleaver under the food, flip it over and repeat the chopping. (You may find holding the blunt end of the cleaver with the left hand and working the handle up and down with the right easier.) Continue doing this until there is an even consistency.

When slicing, you should hold the food with your fingertips tucked well out of the way, your knuckles forward to act as a guide. You should also avoid lifting the blade higher than your knuckles. The blade should be about 2.5 mm (⅛ in) from the edge of the food and you should slice straight downward. The thickness is regulated by moving the fingers further away from the edge being cut.

Slicing thinly is paramount in Oriental cooking because so much of it is stir-fried. Meat can be cut into thin slices, matchstick strips, or cubes; beef should be cut across the grain at a thickness of about 2.5 mm (⅛ in). Stack the slices up and cut them into narrow slivers and you have matchstick strips—ideal for stir-frying, as well as steaming.

Putting meat in the refrigerator for a couple of hours before cutting firms it up and makes it easier to cut neatly (much Oriental cooking does demand a degree of aesthetics not required of other cuisines).

To cut vegetables diagonally, the food should be held from the top with your fingers slanted across at an angle of 60°. Again, using your knuckles as a guide, slice downward. Cutting diagonally gives you more cooking surface and is particularly good for stir-frying. For braising, first make a diagonal cut and then turn the vegetable 90° and cut again. In this way you finish up with chunks that will seal in their own flavour.

ORIENTAL GARNISHING

The Orientals have an intense dislike of using anything that does not have more than one purpose. The ubiquitous spring onion, for example, is never used simply for seasoning, but as a garnish as well. You'd be surprised at how many ways there are of cutting spring onions. They can be cut crosswise in the traditional Western way in slices, diagonally, in lengths, or in threads; alternatively, they can be made into brushes.

SPRING ONION BRUSH

To do this, trim the white ends of the spring onions into 5-cm (2-in) pieces. Using the sharp tip of the cleaver, cut them several times lengthwise from both ends, leaving the middle intact. Place them in a bowl of cold water or water with a couple of ice cubes and put in the refrigerator for several hours. This will curl the ends, giving you the brushes.

CARROT ROSE

The carrot is one of the favourite decorative vegetables of Vietnamese cuisine. To make carrot roses, you will need a carrot about 5 cm (2 in) in diameter. Wash and peel it, cut out a chunk about 5 cm (2 in) thick and place it on a table. Smooth the edges of this chunk to form the shape of a ball, then cut a cross on its top with a knife so that you have four sectors of equal size. Use a sharp knife to cut a petal about 2.5 mm (⅛ in) thick on each of the four sides, stopping about 5 mm (¼ in) from the bottom. Cut around the inside of the first layer of petals to form a groove. Cut a second layer of four petals, positioning them so that the centres of the petals are where those of the first layer end, rather like brickwork. Continue until you can no longer carve petals. Soak the carrot in water until ready to use to garnish.

Alternatively, you can peel and cut a carrot into nine discs about 2 mm (¹⁄₁₀ in) thick. Make a radial cut on each carrot slice and soak the carrot slices in salted water for 2 to 3 minutes to soften them. Dry them and pile three small slices together with the cut sides overlapping to make a cone. Stick a toothpick in the centre and use that as a pistil. Pile the slices around the pistil to form a rose.

CHILLI FLOWERS

Make these by slicing chillies in half from the tip to about 1 cm (½ in) from the bottom. Cut each half into three to give you six petals and separate them from the pistil with a knife. Cut small slants along the edges of each petal and leave the chillies in cold water for at least 2 hours, after which the petals will curl outward to form a flower. Do *not* rub your eyes with your fingers after making a chilli flower.

CUCUMBER FLOWER

Clean and dry the cucumber and slice it evenly down its length. Take one half and slice off the two ends at an angle. Using a small knife, make six very thin slashes, stopping about 5 mm (¼ in) from the other side. Cut through the cucumber at the seventh slash. Curl back every alternate slice and tuck them in firmly so that you have three straight pieces and three curls. Make as many cucumber curls as you like—they will brighten up a dish no end.

Simply carved vegetables add a touch of class to any dish and are regularly used by Thai chefs.

ORANGE WHEELS

You need a couple of oranges. Begin by making a cross on each side of the first orange. Using this cross as a guide, gouge three narrow strips per quarter. Gouge out the center of every strip so that you have 16 in all. Cut the orange lengthwise in half and cut these halves into slices about 2.5 mm (⅛ in) thick. Repeat with the second and set aside. Onions, radishes, tomatoes and the like can be carved in much the same way.

FRUIT WEDGES

Lemons, limes, oranges, apples, peaches, plums and apricots are all suitable. Cut wedges neatly and arrange them in pairs or in threes, either lying on their sides or standing neatly.

CITRUS TWISTS

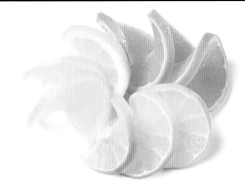

Cut thin slices, then make a slit into the center of each. Move the slit in the fruit in opposite directions to stand the slice up and form the twist.

Attractive presentation of food is very important to Oriental chefs, and a dish's appearance is given as much consideration as the freshness of the ingredients used in it. Decoratively sliced vegetables are chosen for their colours and flavours to complement the dishes they garnish.

BASIC RECIPES

BROWN STOCK

**MAKES ABOUT
3 L (5 PT)**

1 onion, cut into quarters

3 celery sticks, chopped
(use the heart and top as well)

2 cloves

1 clove garlic

4 black peppercorns

1-cm (½-in) piece unpeeled
fresh root ginger

4.25 l (7 pt) water

Place all the ingredients in a large pan and bring to a boil. Adjust the heat to maintain a faint simmer. (It is important to make sure that the stock is not boiled because boiling results in a cloudy broth.)

❀ Simmer for 4 to 5 hours, stirring occasionally. Strain off any foam that rises to the surface.

❀ Leave to cool, then strain. Use as required.

VEGETABLE STOCK

**MAKES ABOUT
1.75 L (3 PT)**

4 carrots, roughly chopped

4 celery sticks, preferably the
heart, tops and leaves,
roughly chopped

3 potatoes, peeled and
quartered

3 spring onions, roughly cut

4 pieces dried wood ears,
soaked for about 30 minutes
and drained

4 black peppercorns

2 cloves

2.5 l (4 pt) water

Place all the ingredients in a pan and bring to a boil. Immediately lower the heat and leave to simmer for 3 hours.

❀ Leave to cool, then strain. Use as required.

CHICKEN STOCK

MAKES ABOUT
3 L (5 PT)

1.5 to 1.75 kg (3 to 4 lb) chicken bones

1-cm (½-in) piece fresh root ginger, peeled and sliced

2 spring onions, halved

4 black peppercorns

4.25 l (7 pt) water

The carcass of a roasted chicken is ideal; thighs, wings and feet also make good stock. After 30 minutes, remove any meat to use in a dish and carry on simmering the bones to give a flavoursome broth.

❀ Place all the ingredients in a pan with a well-fitting lid. Bring to a boil, then immediately reduce the heat to a gentle simmer. Skim off the grey foam until clear.

❀ Bring to the boil again, reducing the heat the moment the first bubbles appear.

❀ Adjust the heat until the stock is just simmering. Cover and leave for 3 to 4 hours.

❀ Leave to cool, then strain and use as required.

FISH STOCK

MAKES ABOUT
900 ML (1½ PT)

1 kg (2 lb) fish bits

1 onion, roughly chopped

1 carrot, roughly chopped

2 celery sticks, roughly chopped

1 clove garlic

4 black peppercorns

1.25 l (2 pt) water

Use any pieces of fish bits, heads and all.

❀ Place all the ingredients in a heavy pan with a tight-fitting lid and bring to a boil.

❀ Reduce the heat immediately and skim off any grey foam that appears until a clear broth is left.

❀ Adjust the heat and leave to simmer for about 3 hours.

❀ Leave to cool, then strain and use as required.

JAPANESE SUSHI

The Japanese have a genius for doing things beautifully. They also have a reputation for making things complicated. Who, for example, has not heard of the Japanese tea ceremony, which elevates a simple enough beverage into an art form?

Sushi can be almost as complicated as the tea ceremony, if you want to go into all the history and learn all the Japanese terms; and certainly, to become a master sushi chef (*itamae*) takes many years. On the other hand, you can learn enough about sushi to make it yourself at home surprisingly quickly. Many Japanese housewives do it all the time—although, of course, they apologize profusely for the fact that it is home-made.

To appreciate sushi at home, you also need to know how to appreciate it when you eat out. There are all kinds of customs that are not immediately obvious: at the most basic, some people eat sushi "set plates" for years before realizing that an *à la carte* order consists of two pieces, not one; or again, that if you are ordering *à la carte*, you do not order all the sushi you want at once. Instead, you order a few pieces, then a few more, and the meal is over when the *itamae* asks you if you want any more, and you say no. By watching the *itamae* you can also learn a great deal about making sushi at home!

It is also worth knowing a little about the history of sushi. One version says the rice was originally used to preserve fish, and was thrown away before the fish was eaten. Some people, however, acquired a taste for this rice, and that was the origin of sushi. Certainly, fermented fish dishes exist in many parts of Asia, including Japan: this is a *nare-zushi* ("sushi" becomes *zushi* when it is hyphenated like this).

Another version, first recorded 1,200 years ago, says the emperor Keiko was once served raw clams with vinegar and liked the taste so much he made the inventor his head chef.

Whatever the truth, there is no doubt sushi is enormously popular, and becoming more popular all the time. Even people who are squeamish about raw fish can become enthusiastic converts, once they realize that sushi rivals the finest fillet steak in texture, and the flavour is exquisite. And, even if they do not want to try the more exotic varieties, such as octopus or sea urchin, they can stick with tuna or yellowtail, vegetarian sushi of various kinds, and even a "kosher" roll made with smoked salmon and cream cheese.

The type of sushi that is best known in the West, and indeed which is most popular in Japan, is called *nigiri-zushi*, or finger sushi. It first became popular about 200 years ago as a fast food—but what an improvement over Western fast food!

Nigiri-zushi is what most people mean when they say "sushi" and in many ways it is the simplest form, at least in concept. The chef carves a piece of raw fish (or any one of a number of other ingredients), puts a smear of wasabi (Japanese horseradish or Japanese mustard) on the bottom and places it on a little finger-shaped patty of vinegared sushi rice. Sometimes, there will be a "strap" of nori (seaweed paper) around it as well. The whole thing is just solid enough to stay together in the fingers or when picked up with chopsticks, but it seems to melt when it is placed in your mouth. Needless to say, this is not quite as easy to prepare as it looks, but it is still something you can learn to do quite satisfactorily at home.

If the topping is soft or semi-liquid, as with some kinds of roe or sea urchin, the sushi chef will build a little "wall" of nori all the way around; such sushi are known as *gunkan-maki*, or battleship sushi from their resemblance to a man-of-war, or battleship.

The next most usual kind of sushi is probably rolled sushi (*maki-zushi*). There are countless varieties of these, and sushi chefs often have specialties which they have developed themselves. At the simplest, though, they consist of a sheet of *nori*, spread with sushi rice. In the centre, the chef puts fish, avocado, cucumber or anything else suitable, then rolls the whole thing up in a tight roll with the help of a flexible bamboo mat. The roll is then cut into slices which in the more expensive restaurants are arranged very artistically.

The most spectacular kinds of rolled sushi may have an additional layer of rice outside the nori, with fish and sometimes avocado rolled on the outside of this. This is where chefs like to show their virtuosity!

A more casual variety of *maki-zushi* is the hand-rolled maki, which usually looks like an old-fashioned ice-cream cone rolled from nori and filled with sushi rice, and whatever takes the fancy of the customer or the sushi chef. Strictly, any *maki* which is not pressed with the bamboo mat is *temaki*.

With any form of rolled sushi, a single roll, which may be cut into anything up to eight pieces, constitutes an order *à la carte*.

Finally, there are various other kinds of finger sushi such as stuffed fried tofu (page 93), Tiger Eye (page 95), and cooked sushi.

SUSHI EQUIPMENT

When you first begin preparing sushi it isn't necessary to use specialist equipment, except for a bamboo rolling mat. But if you find you enjoy sushi-making and intend to do it quite often, it is advisable to buy authentic Japanese cookware from a specialist store.

Ironically, the most important "equipment" for both the novice and the experienced sushi-maker is actually nothing more than running water. This is so you can constantly rinse your hands and knives. A lever-operated tap is much more convenient than an old-fashioned one.

The chopping board (*manaita*) can be of any material: wood is traditional, but plastic works just as well. About 30 x 45 cm (12 x 18 in) is adequate. Because it is hard to remove the smell of fish from a wooden board, reserve one board (or one side of a board) exclusively for cutting fish and shellfish.

A master sushi chef will have a number of knives (*hōchō*). Most of the work is done with three: the all-purpose *banno-bōchō*, the cleaverlike *deba-bōchō* and the square-tipped *nakiri-bōchō* for cutting vegetables. There are, however, many others. Two of the most important, owned by many sushi chefs, are the long, thin *sashimi-bōchō* for slicing boned fillets and the *sushikiri-bōchō* (commonly called *yanagi*).

In practise, a long, fairly light kitchen knife of high quality can be used for most purposes: choose the size (typically a 18- to 25-cm (7- to 10-in blade) that suits you best. Keep the blade razor-sharp; making sushi with blunt knives tears the fish, gives ragged cuts and is generally unsatisfactory. After use, wash and dry the knife and put it away carefully.

A strainer (*zaru*) is essential for draining water off foods. A plastic or enamel colander will do, but a proper bamboo *zaru* is not expensive. It must be dried and aired completely after use, or it will quickly become musty and mouldy.

A rolling mat (*makisu*), an omelette pan, a grater, a fish scaler and thin, round skewers complete the *batterie de cuisine*. A traditional Japanese omelette pan (*tamago-yaki nabe*) is square and about 1.5 cm (¾ in) deep; the shape makes it easier to fold the omelette repeatedly and to cut it into neat strips. Cast-iron pans are traditional, although many cooks use heavy aluminium.

 SUSHI GARNISHING

The line between ingredients and garnishes in sushi can be difficult to draw. After all, a sushi meal is an aesthetic whole. Yet, beautifully cut vegetables for a garnish is an essential part of the Japanese cuisine. Here are a few examples suitable for keen amateur chefs to attempt in their own kitchen.

CUCUMBER PINE-TREE CUT

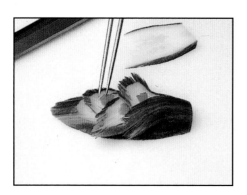

Cut a 6-cm (2½-in) piece off the end of a cucumber, cutting on an angle. Use a thin, sharp knife to slice the end of the cucumber with parallel lines that are equal lengthwise; these slices should be close together and very fine.

Working from the "back" end of the piece of cucumber, hold your knife parallel to the board and make a thin slice from the centre to one side; push the cut portion to the side.

Repeat the slicing process on the other side of the piece of cucumber; push the cut portion to the opposite side from where you pushed the first cut portion.

Repeat the process one more time on each side.

Add a small amount of red fish roe for colour.

DAIKON GARNISHES

Cutting daikon into ornamental shapes is a common practice among sushi makers, and either of these techniques can also be used with a carrot.

The easiest way to produce a flower shape is to use a small biscuit or aspic cutter. Simply peel and cut the daikon into thin slices, then use the cutter to press out a shape.

Another technique involves shaving off a "thick peel," as if you were using a pencil sharpener. The thick peel can then be cut on the bias and will curl attractively.

PICKLED GINGER "ROSE"

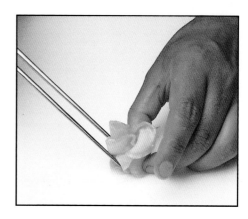

Use a sharp paring knife or a vegetable peeler to peel a long, very thin strip of pickled ginger. Gently roll the delicate strip into a rose shape.

Basic Sushi Recipes

Dashi

**MAKES ABOUT
225 ML (7 FL OZ)**

*5- to 7.5 sq cm (2- to 3-sq-in)
piece seaweed*

225 ml (7 fl oz) cold water

50 g (2 oz) dried bonito flakes

This is one of the fundamental ingredients in Japanese cooking. Although it is encountered less in sushi recipes than other dishes, it is still used in the preparation of several recipes.

Many kinds of Japanese soups are made with dashi as a base, but the two usually encountered with sushi are *suimono* and *miso-dashi*.

❀ To make *suimono*, gently heat dashi with a little tofu but do not boil or the tofu will disintegrate. Add a few flakes of seaweed or a finely chopped spring onion. *Miso-dashi* is made the same way, except it also contains 2 tablespoons miso to each 450 ml (¾ pt) dashi. You can also substitute seasonal vegetables or seafood for tofu.

❀ Put the seaweed and water into a pan over high heat and bring to a boil. As soon as the water boils, remove the seaweed, because leaving it in will make the soup bitter and cloudy.

❀ Add the bonito flakes and turn up the heat but do not stir. As soon as the stock is boiling, remove the pan from the heat. When the bonito flakes sink, the dashi is ready.

❀ Strain out the bonito flakes because leaving them in will make the stock too fishy-tasting. (Both the seaweed and bonito flakes can be re-used again to make a milder stock.)

27

SUSHI RICE

Sushi rice is made from a matured short-grain rice. Some sushi chefs even have their rice merchants mix rice of differing degrees of maturity to achieve the desired result.

❀ Exact quantities are not necessary because sushi rice is best cooked in about its own weight of water: very new rice, which contains more moisture, requires less, and older rice may require more. Experiment to get the best results. You will find it easier if you stick with a single brand of rice, as the moisture content is likely to be more constant.

❀ If you cannot buy the sushi vinegar used in this recipe, dissolve 5 tablespoons sugar in a little more than 5 tablespoons rice vinegar with 2 to 4 teaspoons salt (the higher quantity is more traditional). You will first have to heat the vinegar to get the sugar to dissolve, then cool rapidly by plunging the bowl into cold water, to avoid distilling off the vinegar.

❀ Rinse the rice thoroughly until the water comes clear. Let the rinsed rice dry and swell for an hour.

To cook rice easily, you need a pot with a tight-fitting lid. Bring the rice to a boil over medium heat, then cover tightly.

❀ Boil over high heat for 2 minutes, then over medium heat for 5 minutes, and low heat for about 15 minutes to absorb the remaining water. You should be able to hear the different stages of cooking: at first, the rice bubbles, but when all the water has been absorbed, it begins to hiss. Never remove the lid during cooking if you want the very best rice.

❀ Once the rice has cooked, remove the lid, drape a teatowel over the top of the pan, and let it cool for 10 to 15 minutes.

❀ Pour the rice into a cedarwood rice-cooling tub (*hangiri*) or other nonmetallic container. Spread it out evenly with a rice paddle (*shamoji*) or large wooden spoon.

❀ Run the rice paddle through the rice as though you were plowing a field, first left-to-right and then top-to-bottom, again and again. This is to separate the grains. As you do so, add the sushi vinegar: 150 ml (¼ pt) will treat 675 g to 1 kg (1½ to 2 lb) *uncooked* rice. Do not add too much: the rice should just stick together without being mushy.

❀ At the same time, you need to fan the rice to cool it and help it separate—the action will also add a gloss to the grains. Unless you have three hands, you will need an assistant with a fan or an unromantic but equally effective piece of cardboard. It takes about 10 minutes to get the rice thoroughly mixed and down to room temperature.

Noodle and Rice Dishes

STIR-FRIED NOODLES AND BEANSPROUTS

SERVES 4

1 tbsp vegetable oil

2 small onions, thinly sliced

4 cloves garlic, chopped

110 g (4 oz) beansprouts

175 g (6 oz) (dried weight) cellophane noodles, soaked in warm water for 30 minutes, drained and cut into 7.5-cm (3-in) pieces

125 ml (4 fl oz) chicken stock

1 tbsp light soy sauce

2 spring onions, thinly sliced

1 tbsp chopped fresh coriander

freshly ground black pepper

Heat the oil in a wok over high heat. Add the onions and garlic and fry for 2 minutes or so until the edges begin to brown.

❀ Add the beansprouts and stir-fry for 30 seconds. Add the noodles. Stir-fry for 1 minute.

❀ Stir in the chicken stock and soy sauce, and toss to combine.

❀ Add the spring onions and remove from heat. Serve on a serving dish with coriander and black pepper sprinkled all over.

STIR-FRIED VERMICELLI WITH VEGETABLES

SERVES 4

1 tbsp vegetable oil

1 clove garlic, finely chopped

1 carrot, thinly sliced

60 ml (4 tbsp) water

50 g (2 oz) Chinese cabbage, shredded

½ celery stick, shredded

3 tbsp chicken stock

1 tbsp oyster sauce

1 tbsp light soy sauce and ½ tsp anchovy extract

1 tsp sugar

freshly ground black pepper

100–125 g (4 oz) rice vermicelli, soaked in warm water for 5 minutes and drained well

Heat the oil in a wok over high heat. Add the garlic and stir-fry until golden brown. Add the carrot and stir-fry for 1 minute.

❀ Add all the remaining ingredients, except the vermicelli, stirring gently. Continue stir-frying for 2 minutes.

❀ Add the vermicelli and toss to combine all the ingredients. Stir-fry for 1 minute longer. Serve in a large serving dish.

CASSEROLED PRAWNS WITH "GLASS" NOODLES

SERVES 6

2 slices bacon, cut into
2-cm (1-in) pieces

6 raw large prawns, shelled

2 coriander roots, cut in half

25 g (1 oz) fresh root ginger,
pounded or finely chopped

2 tbsp chopped garlic

1 tbsp white peppercorns,
crushed

450 g (16 oz) cellophane
noodles, soaked in cold water for
10 minutes and well drained

1 tsp butter

3 tbsp black soy sauce

60 ml (4 tbsp) roughly chopped
coriander leaves and stems

SOUP STOCK

450 ml (¾ pt) chicken stock

2 tbsp oyster sauce

2 tbsp black soy sauce

½ tbsp sesame seed oil

1 tsp brandy or whisky

½ tsp sugar

Place all the soup stock ingredients in a pan. Bring to a boil, then lower the heat and simmer for 5 minutes. Leave to cool.

❀ Place the bacon over the bottom of a flameproof casserole. Add the prawns, coriander root, ginger, garlic and peppercorns. Place the noodles over the top, then add the butter, soy sauce and soup stock.

❀ Place on the heat and cover. Bring to a boil, then lower the heat and simmer for 5 minutes. Mix well with tongs, add the coriander, cover and cook again for about 5 minutes until the prawns turn pink. Remove excess stock liquid before serving.

FRIED THAI NOODLES WITH CHILLIES AND VEGETABLES

SERVES 4

175 g (6 oz) instant dried noodles

2 tbsp sunflower oil

2 lemon grass stalks, chopped and outer leaves removed

2.5-cm (1-in) piece fresh root ginger, peeled and grated

1 red onion, cut into thin wedges

2 garlic cloves, crushed

4 red bird's-eye chillies, seeded and sliced

1 red pepper, seeded and cut into matchsticks

1 small carrot, very thinly sliced with a vegetable peeler

1 small courgette, trimmed and sliced with a vegetable peeler

85 g (3 oz) mange tout, trimmed and cut diagonally in half

6 spring onions, trimmed and diagonally sliced

100–125 g (4 oz) cashew nuts

2 tbsp soy sauce

juice of 1 orange

1 tsp honey

1 tbsp sesame oil

Rice or noodles, whether boiled or fried, form the basis of most meals in Thailand. Thai cooking is often pungent and hot but at the same time is slightly perfumed. This is often due to the lemon grass which features strongly in most of their dishes.

✿ Cook the noodles in lightly salted boiling water for 3 minutes. Drain, and plunge them into cold water, then drain again; reserve.

✿ Heat the oil in a wok or large pan. Add the lemon grass and ginger and stir-fry for 2 minutes.

Discard the lemon grass and ginger, keeping the oil in the pan.

✿ Add the onion, garlic and chillies and stir-fry for 2 minutes longer. Add the red pepper and cook for 2 minutes longer.

✿ Add the remaining vegetables and continue stir-frying for 2 minutes. Then add the reserved noodles and cashew nuts with the soy sauce, orange juice and honey.

✿ Stir-fry for 1 minute. Add the sesame oil and stir-fry for 30 seconds. Serve immediately.

33

CHOW MEIN

SERVES 4

25 g (1 oz) dried tofu skin sticks, soaked overnight in cold water and drained

100–125 g (4 oz) fresh spinach or any other greens, finely shredded

225 g (8 oz) dried egg noodles

3 to 4 tbsp oil

2 spring onions, thinly shredded

2 tbsp light soy sauce

50 g (2 oz) dried tiger lily buds, soaked overnight in cold water and drained

50 g (2 oz) bamboo shoots, finely shredded

1 tsp salt

2 tsp sesame seed oil

After chop suey, chow mein, which means "fried noodles" in Chinese, must be the next most popular dish in Chinese restaurants. Try to get freshly made noodles from an Oriental food store or Italian delicatessen, because they taste much better than dried ones. As a rough guide, allow at least 50 g (2 oz) dried noodles per person and double the weight if using freshly made ones. You will have to look in Oriental food stores for many of these ingredients.

❀ Thinly shred the tofu skins and tiger lily buds.

❀ Cook the noodles in a pan of boiling water according to the instructions on the package. Depending on the thickness of the noodles, this should take 5 minutes or so; freshly made noodles will take only about half that time.

❀ Heat about half the oil in a hot wok or pan. While waiting for it to smoke, drain the noodles. Add them with about half the spring onions and the soy sauce to the wok and stir-fry; do not overcook or the noodles will become soggy. Remove and place them on a serving dish.

❀ Add the rest of the oil to the wok. When hot, add the other spring onions and stir a few times. Then add all the vegetables and continue stirring.

❀ After 30 seconds or so, add the salt and the remaining soy sauce together with a little water if necessary. As soon as the sauce starts to boil, add the sesame seed oil and blend everything well. Place the mixture on top of the fried noodles as a dressing.

Chow Mein

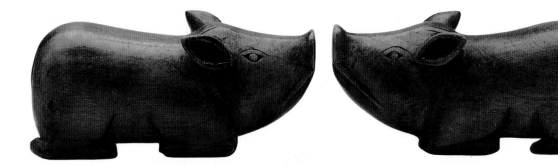

PLAIN RICE

SERVES 4

400 g (14 oz) long-grained white rice

600 ml (1 pt) water

1 tsp salt

The Vietnamese believe that the way to cook perfect rice is never to lift the lid while it is boiling.

❁ Rinse the rice several times until the water runs clear. Drain properly and place in a saucepan. Add the water and salt. Bring to a boil. Lower the heat until it is just bubbling gently, cover, and leave to cook for about 20 minutes. After 20 minutes, lift the cover and test to see if the rice is done to perfection.

❁ Turn off the heat, cover the saucepan once more, and leave for about 10 minutes to give the rice time to absorb all the moisture. Serve at once.

SHRIMP-FRIED RICE

SERVES 4

2 tbsp vegetable oil

450 g (1 lb) raw prawns,
shelled

1 spring onion, chopped

50 g (2 oz) fresh button
mushrooms

1 courgette, thinly sliced

½ carrot, thinly sliced

110 g (4 oz) green beans cut
into 2-cm (1-in) pieces

1 tbsp rice wine or dry sherry

1 tsp light soy sauce

freshly ground black pepper

salt

200 g (7 oz) plain boiled rice

2 spring onions, neatly chopped
to garnish

Heat ½ tablespoon oil in a wok. Add the
shrimp and stir-fry for 1 minute; set aside.
❁ Add the remaining oil and spring onion and
cook until it softens. Add the mushrooms and the
other vegetables and stir-fry for 2 minutes over
high heat.
❁ Put the prawns back into the wok. Add the
vegetables and the rest of the ingredients, except
the rice, stir-frying constantly.
❁ Add the rice and stir-fry until the rice has
changed colour. Place in a large serving bowl and
garnish with the chopped spring onions.

STICKY RICE

SERVES 4

400 g (14 oz) short-grain glutinous rice (specified on package)

1 tsp salt

In Vietnam, sticky rice is often served at breakfast, which is convenient because the rice should be soaked for at least 8 hours. There are two ways of preparing it and both are described below. Unlike Westerners, Vietnamese save the rice crust at the bottom of the saucepan for a variety of purposes: to dip in sauces, to deep-fry, and to eat between meals in much the same way as Americans eat biscuits.

METHOD 1

✿ Rinse and drain the rice after soaking overnight. Spread the soaked rice mixed with the salt over dampened muslin in the top of a steamer and steam for about 40 minutes, sprinkling water over it occasionally. Taste while cooking for consistency. It should be very tender.

METHOD 2

✿ Boil about 750 ml (1¼ pt) water in a heavy-bottomed saucepan. Add the rice and salt and bring it back to a boil. Let it boil for 1 minute or so and then cover it with a well-fitting lid. Take it off the heat and hold the lid tightly on the saucepan. Turn it over and drain until fairly dry.

✿ Place over very low heat and let the rice cook for about 20 minutes. After cooking, set it aside for 10 minutes to complete the cooking. When ready to serve, fluff it up with a fork or chopsticks.

PERFUMED RICE

SERVES 4

450 ml (¾ pt) Thai perfumed rice

600 m l (1 pt) water

1 tsp salt

Although some Thai rice is described as "perfumed" on the bag, most people are rightly unable to detect the fragrance.

✿ Rinse the rice several times and drain; when the water is clear, the rice is as clean as it can possibly be.

✿ Put the rice and water in a saucepan. Add the salt and bring quickly to a boil. Reduce the heat immediately and cover. Let simmer for as long as necessary—30 minutes is about right. The rice should be taken off the heat and left to rest for about 10 minutes before serving. The result should be a rather moist, slightly sticky boiled rice that people east of the Ganges prefer.

CHICKEN-FRIED RICE

SERVES 4

3 tbsp peanut or corn oil

200 g (7 oz) boneless skinned chicken breasts, cut lengthwise into 1-cm (½-in) thick slices

1 tbsp chopped garlic

1 onion, sliced

2 eggs

225 g (8 oz) cooked long-grain rice

1 tomato, cut into 8 wedges

1 spring onion, chopped

2 tsp white soy sauce

1 tsp fish sauce

1 tsp sugar

1 tsp ground white pepper

This always tastes best with rice from the day before—and is easier to cook if the rice has been chilled for a while. In place of chicken, pork or shrimp are also commonly used.

❀ Heat the oil in a wok or pan. Add the chicken and garlic and stir-fry for 1 minute.

❀ Add the onion and cook for 1 minute.

❀ Break in the eggs, mix very well and then stir in the rice and the rest of the ingredients. Stir-fry for 2 minutes.

❀ Serve immediately accompanied by cucumber slices, whole spring onions.

PINEAPPLE AND CHILLI RICE

SERVES 4

1 large or 2 medium fresh pineapple

2 tbsp sunflower oil

1 red pepper, seeded and chopped

110 g (4 oz) trimmed and diced courgettes

6 spring onions, trimmed and sliced diagonally

110 g (4 oz) cooked long-grain rice

6 tinned jalapeño chillies, drained and chopped

salt and pepper

2 tbsp pine nuts, toasted

3 tbsp freshly chopped coriander

grated cheese to serve

Cut the pineapple in half lengthwise through the plume and scoop out the flesh. Reserve the halves. Discard the central core, dice the remaining flesh and reserve.

❀ Heat the oil in a wok or pan. Add the red pepper and courgettes and stir-fry for 5 minutes, or until softened. Add the spring onions and stir-fry for 1 minute.

❀ Stir in the rice with the chillies, seasoning and the reserved pineapple flesh.

❀ Heat gently, stirring occasionally, for 5 minutes, or until hot. Then stir in the pine nuts and coriander. Pile into the reserved pineapple shells and serve with grated cheese.

FRIED RICE WITH SPICY SAUCE

SERVES 4 TO 6

2 tbsp peanut oil

225 g (8 oz) cooked long-grain rice

3 tbsp phrik nam plaa sauce

PHRIK NAM PLAA SAUCE

60 ml (4 tbsp) fish sauce

10 small green chillies, sliced

1 tsp sliced shallot

¼ tsp palm sugar

1 tbsp lemon or lime juice

To make the sauce, combine all the ingredients. Set aside. (This is a good accompaniment to most Thai food, especially rice. Just sprinkle a little on top to liven the food up.)

❁ Heat the oil in a wok or pan. Add the rice and mix well, stir-frying for 1 minute.

❁ Add the sauce, mix well and stir-fry for 1 minute longer. Remove from the heat.

❁ Serve accompanied by preserved salted eggs, cucumber slices, fried eggs and raw vegetables.

EGG FRIED RICE

2 eggs

2 tbsp water

2 tbsp vegetable oil

2 spring onions, finely chopped

300 g (11 oz) plain boiled rice

2 tbsp soy sauce

salt

½ tsp sugar

Pre-cooked, but cold rice works well when fried. This is a simple, yet tasty, way to make good use of left-over plain rice.

❀ Beat the eggs with the water in a bowl.

❀ Heat ½ teaspoon oil in a hot wok and add the egg mixture. Swirl it around to make an omelette. Transfer to a plate and allow to cool. When cool, cut into strips.

❀ Heat the remaining oil. Add the spring onions and stir-fry for 2 minutes. Add the plain boiled rice and omelette strips.

❀ Stir in the soy sauce, salt and sugar. Continue stir-frying for 2 to 3 minutes. Serve in a bowl.

CHICKEN RICE

300 g (11 oz) boneless skinned capon or chicken meat

1.25 l (2 pt) water

3 coriander roots

2 tsp salt

225 g (8 oz) long-grain rice, rinsed

10 garlic cloves, chopped

15 g (½ oz) fresh root ginger, peeled, sliced and crushed

3 tbsp peanut or corn oil

12.5-cm (5-in) piece of cucumber, cut into 5 mm (¼-in) slices

60 ml (4 tbsp) coriander leaves

KHAO MAN SAUCE

5 fresh small green chillies, chopped

2 tbsp pickled soya beans

½ tbsp chopped root ginger

½ tbsp white vinegar

1 tsp sugar

1 tsp soy sauce

¼ tsp chopped garlic

A very popular day-time dish that is Chinese in origin. The special feature is that the rice is cooked in chicken broth (ideally, capon). The chicken pieces are always arranged on top of the mound of rice.

❀ Bring the water to a boil. Add the chicken, coriander root and salt, and simmer about 15 minutes until the chicken is tender. Remove the meat with a slotted spoon and put to one side.

❀ Strain the cooking liquid. Put 900 ml (1½ pt) back in the pan and add the rice, garlic, ginger and oil. Bring back to a boil, cover and simmer for 15 to 18 minutes until the rice is tender and all the liquid absorbed.

❀ Place the rice on serving plates. Slice the chicken across into 1 cm (½-in) pieces and place on top of the hot rice. Arrange the cucumber slices around the sides and sprinkle with the coriander leaves.

❀ Mix all the ingredients for the sauce together in a bowl. Serve with the chicken and rice, and with the remaining chicken cooking liquid.

SOUPS AND APPETIZERS

CHICKEN PHO

SERVES 4

3 celery sticks, finely chopped

3 spring onions, chopped (use green tops as well)

335 g (12 oz) finely shredded cooked chicken meat

225 g (8 oz) banh pho or rice stick noodles

900 ml (1½ pt) chicken stock

2 pieces dried wood ears or 8 white button mushrooms, finely sliced

Traditionally, Vietnamese pho is only made with beef. It is a sign of the times, however, that it is now made with chicken and prawns.

❁ Place the celery and spring onions in a bowl and put on the table. Place the cooked shredded chicken in a separate bowl and put that on the table also.

❁ Follow the cooking instructions on the noodle package or boil the noodles until just tender. Drain and rinse with some boiling water. Place in 4 bowls.

❁ Boil the chicken stock until it is simmering. Add the mushrooms. Place in a bowl and put on the table.

❁ To serve, the guests should put a mixture of celery, spring onions and shredded chicken onto the noodles, then ladle the hot chicken stock into the bowls.

CHINESE CABBAGE SOUP

SERVES 3 TO 4

3 to 4 dried Chinese mushrooms, soaked in warm water for 30 minutes

2 tbsp vegetable oil

250 g (9 oz) Chinese cabbage, thinly sliced

2 tsp salt

1 tbsp rice wine or dry sherry

900 ml (1½ pt) water

1 tsp sesame oil

Squeeze dry the soaked mushrooms. Discard the hard stems and cut the mushrooms into small pieces; reserve the water in which the mushrooms have been soaked for use later.

❀ Heat a wok or large pan until hot. Add oil and wait for it to smoke. Add the cabbage and mushrooms. Stir a few times and then add the salt, wine, water and the mushroom soaking water. Bring to a boil, add the sesame oil, and serve.

HOT-AND-SOUR SOUP

SERVES 3 TO 4

900 ml (1½ pt) water

3 dried Chinese mushrooms, soaked in warm water for 30 minutes

2 cakes tofu, thinly shredded

50 g (2 oz) Szechwan preserved vegetables, drained and thinly shredded

50 g (2 oz) pickled vegetables, such as cucumber, cabbage or green beans, drained and thinly shredded

2 spring onions, finely chopped

2 slices fresh root ginger, thinly shredded

1 tsp salt

2 tbsp rice wine or sherry

1 tbsp soy sauce

freshly ground pepper to taste

1 tsp sesame oil

1 tsp cornflour mixed with 2 tsp water

A little vinegar can be added to this soup if you find the pickled vegetables do not give a sour enough taste.

❀ Squeeze dry the mushrooms after soaking. Discard the hard stems and cut mushrooms into thin shreds; reserve the water for use later.

❀ Bring the water to the boil in a wok or large pan. Add all the ingredients and seasonings and simmer for 2 minutes. Add the sesame oil and thicken the soup by stirring in the cornflour and water mixture. Serve hot!

CORN AND ASPARAGUS SOUP

SERVES 2 TO 3

600 ml (1 pt) water

1 tsp salt

110 g (4 oz) corn kernels, well drained

175 g (6 oz) white asparagus, finely cubed

1 egg white, lightly beaten

1 tbsp cornflour mixed with 2 tbsp water to make a smooth paste

1 spring onion, finely chopped, to garnish

B ring the water to a rolling boil. Add the salt, corn and asparagus.

❀ When the water starts to boil again, add the cornflour and water mixture, stirring constantly.

❀ Add the egg white very slowly and stir. Serve hot, garnished with finely chopped spring onions.

Coconut and Galangal Soup

SERVES 4 TO 6

1.25 l (2 pt) thin coconut milk

2 tbsp finely chopped shallot

15 g (½ oz) galangal, thinly sliced

2 stalks lemon grass, cut into 15-cm (¾-in) pieces

6 fresh, small whole red chillies

3 kaffir lime leaves, torn into small pieces

1 tsp salt

300 g (11 oz) boneless skinned chicken breasts, cut across into 5-mm (¼-in) slices

200 g (7 oz) fresh mushrooms, oyster if available

2 tbsp lime or lemon juice

½ tbsp fish sauce

3 tbsp coriander leaves and stems cut into 1.5-cm (¾-in) pieces

This creamy soup has become one of the favourites on Thai restaurant menus, not least for the delicate aroma and flavour given by the galangal. Although rather like ginger in appearance, it is much milder and more fragrant.

❈ Pour the coconut milk into a pan and bring to a boil. Add the shallot, galangal, lemon grass, chilli, lime leaf and salt.

❈ Bring to a boil, add the chicken. Bring to a boil again, then add the mushrooms and bring back to a boil for 2 minutes.

❈ Remove from the heat and stir in the lime juice, fish sauce and coriander.

❈ Serve in bowls accompanied by rice and lime quarters.

DEEP-FRIED TOFU AND WOOD EARS SOUP

SERVES 2 TO 3

1 cake fresh tofu, cut into about 20 small cubes

vegetable oil for deep-frying

15 g (½ oz) wood ears (dried mushrooms)

600 ml (1 pt) water

1 tsp salt

1 tbsp light soy sauce

1 spring onion, finely chopped

1 tsp sesame oil

Deep-fry the tofu cubes in very hot vegetable oil until they are puffed up and golden. Drain well, then cut them in half.

❁ Meanwhile, soak the wood ears in water for 20 to 25 minutes until soft. Rinse well.

❁ Bring the water to the boil in a wok or large pan. Add the tofu, wood ears and the salt.

❁ When the soup starts to boil again, add the soy sauce and simmer for about 1 minute.

❁ Garnish with finely chopped spring onion and sesame oil. Serve hot.

Dried Tofu Skin and Vermicelli Soup

SERVES 3 TO 4

15 g (½ oz) dried tofu skin

25 g (1 oz) dried lily buds

8 g (¼ oz) black moss

900 ml (1½ pt) water

50 g (2 oz) cellophane vermicelli
noodles, cut into short pieces

1 tsp salt

2 tbsp light soy sauce

1 tbsp rice wine or dry sherry

1 tsp finely chopped fresh root
ginger

2 spring onions, finely chopped

2 tsp sesame oil

fresh coriander to garnish

S oak the tofu skin in hot water for 30–35
minutes, then drain and cut it into small
pieces.

❁ Soak the lily buds and black moss in water
separately for 20 to 25 minutes. Rinse the lily buds
until clean. Loosen the black moss until it
resembles human hair.

❁ Bring the water to a boil in a wok or large
saucepan. Add all the ingredients, except the
sesame oil and garnish. Stir until well blended.

❁ Cook the soup for 1 to 1½ minutes. Add the
sesame oil and serve hot, garnished with
coriander leaves.

NOODLE SOUP

SERVES 4

200 g (7 oz) pork tenderloin, cut into thin slices

425 g (15 oz) thin rice vermicelli noodles

175 g (6 oz) beansprouts

100–125 g (4 oz) pork liver, boiled and sliced thinly

1 tsp chopped Chinese preserved cabbage

2.5 l (4 pt) chicken stock

12 fish balls

110 g (4 oz) minced pork

1 spring onion, cut into 1-cm (½-in) pieces

2 tbsp coriander leaves and stems, cut into 1-cm (½-in) pieces

2 tbsp chopped garlic, fried in oil until golden

½ tsp ground white pepper

Very much a quick daytime dish, this soup is of Chinese origin but served all over Thailand—on the rivers and canals you can still see floating kwitiaow vendors in small, especially kitted-out boats. The ingredients vary from place to place, although fish balls are normally a constant. This version contains three varieties of pork. Serve accompanied by fish sauce, chilli powder, sugar and sliced fresh red chillies in vinegar, all in separate bowls. Add these according to individual taste.

❁ Boil the pork tenderloin for about 15 minutes. Remove it from the heat, set aside on a plate. When it has cooled slightly, cut into 1 cm (½-in) thick strips; keep the strips on one side.

❁ Cook the noodles and beansprouts together lightly in boiling water for 3 minutes—don't cook until very soft. Drain and place in deep soup bowls, with the beansprouts underneath. Place the sliced pork, liver and preserved cabbage on top of the noodles.

❁ Bring the chicken stock to a boil. Add the fish balls and boil for 3 minutes. Remove with a slotted spoon and add to the bowls.

❁ Put the ground pork in a small pan with 375 ml (12 fl oz) of the chicken stock and heat gently for 4 to 5 minutes, mixing well until the pork is cooked. Add the spring onion, coriander, garlic and pepper. Pour into the bowls. Top with more chicken stock as needed to fill each bowl.

THAI SEAFOOD SOUP

1.5 l (2½ pt) chicken stock

150 g (5 oz) sea bass or other firm fish, cleaned, gutted, and cut into 6 pieces

5 raw large prawns, shelled

1 blue crab, cleaned, shell removed, and chopped into 6 pieces

6 mussels in their shells, cleaned well

150 g (5 oz) squid, body and tentacles, cleaned, gutted and cut into 1.5-cm (¾-in) pieces

2 stalks of lemon grass, cut into 5-cm (2-in) pieces and crushed

60 ml (4 tbsp) sliced galangal

3 kaffir lime leaves, shredded

25 g (1 oz) sweet basil leaves

8 fresh small green chillies, crushed lightly

5 dried red chillies, fried lightly

2½ tbsp fish sauce, or to taste

¼ tsp sugar

1 tbsp lime or lemon juice, or to taste

Treat the ingredients listed here as a guideline.

❁ Use whatever is available at the fishmongers, but try to assemble a variety of textures and flavours: the more the better. Serve in bowls accompanied by rice and extra fish sauce and lime or lemon juice.

❁ Pour the chicken stock into a wok or pan and bring to a boil. Add all the seafood. Then add the lemon grass, galangal and lime leaves. Boil, add all the rest of the ingredients, and simmer for 2 minutes longer.

❁ Remove from the heat. Taste and add more fish sauce or lime juice to taste.

HOT-AND-SOUR PRAWN SOUP

900 ml (1½ pt) fish or chicken stock

2 lemon grass stalks

2-cm (1-in) piece root ginger, peeled and grated

2 or 3 bird's-eye chillies, seeded and chopped

few fresh kaffir lime leaves

1 large carrot, cut into julienne strips

450 g (1 lb) raw large prawns, shelled and deveined

100–125 g (4 oz) wiped and sliced shiitake mushrooms

2 tbsp lime juice

1 tbsp fish sauce

1 tsp chili paste

100 g (4 oz) beansprouts

2 tbsp freshly chopped coriander

This is a very fragrant soup from Thailand. Some recipes use tamarind to give the sour taste, others, like this one, use the more easily available lime juice.

❋ Put the stock into a large pan. Remove the outer leaves from the lemon grass and finely chop. Add to the stock with the ginger, chillies and lime leaves. Bring to a boil, then lower the heat and simmer for 10 minutes.

❋ Add the carrot, prawns and mushrooms to the pan. Simmer for 5 to 8 minutes longer, or until the shrimp have turned pink.

❋ Mix the lime juice, fish sauce and chilli paste together, then stir into the pan and continue simmering for 1 to 2 minutes. Add the beansprouts and chopped coriander, stir once and then serve.

CHINESE MUSHROOM SOUP

SERVES 2 TO 3

6 dried Chinese mushrooms, soaked in warm water for 30 minutes

2 tsp cornflour

1 tbsp cold water

3 egg whites

2 tsp salt

600 ml (1 pt) water

1 spring onion, finely chopped

Squeeze the mushrooms dry after soaking. Discard the hard stems and cut each mushroom into thin slices; reserve the water in which the mushrooms were soaked for use later.

✿ Mix the cornflour with the water to make a smooth paste. Comb the egg whites with your fingers to loosen them.

✿ Mix the water and the mushroom soaking water in a saucepan and bring to the boil. Add the mushrooms and cook for about 1 minute.

✿ Add the cornflour and water mixture, stir, and add the salt.

✿ Pour the egg whites very slowly into the soup, stirring constantly.

✿ Garnish with the finely chopped spring onions and serve hot.

ORIENTAL CUCUMBER SOUP

SERVES 3 TO 4

600 ml (1 pt) water

*½ cucumber, halved lengthwise
and thinly sliced*

*50 g (2 oz) black field
mushrooms, sliced*

1½ tsp salt

1 tsp sesame oil

1 spring onion, finely chopped

Bring the water to a boil in a wok or large saucepan. Add the cucumber and mushroom slices and salt. Boil for about 1 minute.

❀ Add the sesame oil and finely chopped spring onion. Stir and serve hot.

TOMATO AND EGG FLOWER SOUP

SERVES 4 TO 5

250 g (9 oz) tomatoes

1 egg, lightly beaten

2 spring onions, finely chopped

1 tbsp vegetable oil

900 ml (1½ pt) water

2 tbsp light soy sauce

1 tsp cornflour mixed to a smooth paste with 2 tsp water

Skin the tomatoes by dipping them in boiling water for a minute or so, then skin them. Cut into large slices.

❀ Heat a wok or saucepan over high heat. Add the oil and wait for it to smoke. Add the spring onions to flavour the oil, then pour in the water.

❀ Drop in the tomatoes and bring to a boil. Add the soy sauce and very slowly pour in the beaten egg.

❀ Add the cornflour-and-water mixture. Stir and serve.

BEANSPROUT SOUP

SERVES 2 TO 3

225 g (8 oz) fresh beansprouts

2 tbsp vegetable oil

1 small red bell pepper, cored, seeded and thinly shredded

2 tsp salt

600 ml (1 pt) water

1 spring onion, finely chopped

Rinse the beansprouts in cold water, discarding the husks and other bits and pieces that float to the surface. It is not necessary to trim each sprout.

❀ Heat a wok or large saucepan. Add the oil and wait for it to smoke. Add the beansprouts and red pepper and stir a few times. Add the salt and water.

❀ When the soup starts to boil, garnish with finely chopped spring onion and serve hot.

Prawns with Sesame Seeds on Toast

SERVES 4 TO 5

4 tbsp white sesame seeds	1 small egg, beaten
½ tbsp dried shrimp (optional)	salt and freshly ground black pepper
335 g (12 oz) peeled prawns, chopped	
	cornflour for dusting
2 cloves garlic, crushed and chopped	1 thin French stick or 8 slices bread, crusts cut off
½ tsp grated fresh root ginger	vegetable oil for deep-frying
1 small onion, grated	

Toast the sesame seeds in a dry pan until they begin to brown, shaking frequently to prevent them burning.

❀ If using dried shrimp, soak them in warm water until soft. Drain thoroughly and squeeze out excess water. Chop them finely.

❀ Combine the dried and fresh prawns, garlic, ginger, grated onion, egg, salt and black pepper, and knead together with your hands. The mixture should be stiff but not too stiff to spread. If it is too runny, dust with the cornflour.

❀ Cut the French bread into 1-cm (½-in) slices or cut the slices of bread into triangles or shape using pastry cutters.

❀ Press the sesame seeds firmly into the mixture. Using the back of a spoon spread the mixture firmly onto the bread. Refrigerate for at least 2 hours.

❀ Heat enough oil in a wok or deep pan to just deep-fry the rounds, prawn side down, for 1 minute. Using a spatula, turn them over carefully and fry the other side for 1 minute longer. Drain well on absorbent kitchen paper and serve hot.

THAI HORS D'OEUVRE

75 ml (5 tbsp) unsweetened grated coconut, toasted until light brown

3 tbsp finely diced shallots

3 tbsp finely diced lime

3 tbsp diced fresh root ginger

3 tbsp chopped dried shrimp

3 tbsp unsalted roasted peanuts

2 tsp chopped fresh green chillies

1 lettuce or bunch of edible vegetable leaves

SAUCE

2 tbsp unsweetened grated coconut

½ tbsp shrimp paste

½ tsp sliced galangal

½ tsp sliced shallot

3 tbsp chopped unsalted peanuts

2 tbsp chopped dried shrimp

1 tsp sliced ginger

225 g (8 oz) sugar

600 ml (1 pt) water

❀ First, make the sauce. Roast the coconut, shrimp paste, galangal and shallot in a preheated 180°C/350°F/Gas Mark 4 oven for 5 minutes until fragrant; let cool. Place with the peanuts, shrimp, and ginger in a blender or food processor and finely chop, or pound with a pestle and mortar until fine.

❀ Transfer the mixture into a heavy-bottomed saucepan with the sugar and water. Mix well and bring to a boil, then lower the heat and simmer until it is reduced to about 300 ml (½ pt). Remove from the heat and leave to cool.

❀ To serve, pour the sauce into a serving bowl and arrange the remaining ingredients in separate piles on a platter or in small bowls.

❀ To eat, take a lettuce leaf, place a small amount of each of the garnishes in the middle, top with a spoonful of sauce and fold up into a package.

A hard-to-find treat in Thailand, but always enjoyed. The Thais use fresh tree and grape leaves, but this recipe substitutes lettuce. A dish well worth the trouble to prepare.

STUFFED CHICKEN WINGS

SERVES 4

8 chicken wings

STUFFING

100–125 g (4 oz) cellophane noodles

3 pieces dried wood ears

225g (8 oz) minced pork

1 small onion, finely grated

1 small carrot, finely grated

1 egg, beaten

1 tbsp nuoc mam sauce (page 72) or light soy sauce

salt and black pepper

Bone the chicken wings by cutting around the bone with a sharp knife. Holding the wingtip, gently ease the bone away to leave the skin and a thin layer of chicken.

❉ Soak the noodles in warm water for 10 minutes, then drain thoroughly and cut into short strands.

❉ Soak the wood ears in warm water for 30 minutes, then squeeze dry and chop into thin slices.

❉ Mix all the stuffing ingredients together; the mixture should be firm. Mould the stuffing into a ball and insert it into the bag of flesh and skin of the chicken wings.

❉ Preheat the oven to 200°C/400°F/Gas Mark 6. Steam the stuffed wings for 10 to 15 minutes. (If you want to make a large quantity, multiply the measures accordingly and freeze after the steaming stage.)

❉ After steaming, place in a lightly oiled roasting tin and roast in the oven for 30 minutes. Serve on

FISH CRYSTAL EGG ROLLS

1 fresh red snapper, sea bass, or carp, cleaned and gutted

2 tsp salt

5 tbsp dry sherry

1½ tbsp cornflour

vegetable oil

175 g (6 oz) rice noodles

2 pickled gherkins, chopped

2 pickled onions, chopped

1 carrot, grated

1 package round rice paper

DIPPING SAUCE

4 tbsp nuoc mam sauce (page 72)

1 red chilli, finely chopped

1 clove garlic, finely chopped

1 tbsp lemon juice

1 tsp cider vinegar or wine vinegar

1 tsp sugar

2 tsp dry sherry

TO SERVE

sprigs of coriander

sprigs of mint

1 Webbs lettuce

Make slanting slashes down both sides of the fish, about 1.5 cm (¾ in) apart. Mix the salt, sherry and 1 tablespoon cornflour in a dish large enough to contain the fish. Roll the fish in this mixture until well coated and then leave to stand for 30 minutes, turning several times.

❀ Remove the fish from the dish and dust with the remaining cornflour.

❀ Heat the oil in a pan big enough to hold the fish and fry over medium heat for about 12 minutes, turning once, very gently. Drain on absorbent kitchen paper; keep the fish warm as you assemble the other ingredients.

❀ Soak the rice noodles in warm water until soft. Drain thoroughly.

❀ Combine all the ingredients for the dipping sauce and mix together. Toss the gherkins, onions, and carrot into the rice noodles.

❀ Assemble all the components on the table. The fish should be warm and gently scraped away from the bones. Provide two bowls of warm water for dipping the rice papers in.

❀ The guests help themselves to a round rice paper. This is dipped into the warm water and removed before it disintegrates; it should be soft and pliable. The fish, rice noodles, mint and coriander are placed on the rice paper. It is then rolled up to a pencil shape and placed on a piece of lettuce. A lettuce leaf is then rolled around the egg roll and dipped into the dipping sauce.

PRAWNS CRYSTAL EGG ROLLS

SERVES 4

4 uncooked boneless pork slices

3 tbsp honey

2 tbsp dry sherry

1 tsp chilli powder

225 g (8 oz) rice vermicelli

450 g (1 lb) fresh prawns, cooked and halved

225 g (8 oz) finely chopped cooked chicken

3 pickled onions, cut into fine strips

3 dill pickles, cut into fine strips

1 carrot, grated

1 package round rice paper

DIPPING SAUCE

125 ml (4 fl oz) nuoc mam sauce (page 72)

1 red chilli pepper, finely chopped

1 clove garlic, finely chopped

2 to 3 tbsp lemon juice

2 tsp wine vinegar

2 tsp ginger wine

1 tsp sugar

TO SERVE

1 butterhead lettuce

sprigs of coriander

sprigs of mint

To make the cold crispy pork, take the four slices of fresh boneless pork. Mix the honey, dry sherry and chilli powder together. Spread the mixture over the pork. Let rest for 1 hour or longer if possible.

❉ Broil the pork slices until really crisp, turning once so they are evenly cooked. Leave to cool, then cut into thin strips.

❉ Make the dipping sauce by combining all the ingredients and mixing thoroughly; set aside.

❉ Soak the rice vermicelli in boiled water, slightly cooled. When soft, drain and leave to cool.

❉ Place a clean teatowel on the surface you are working on. Dip single sheets of rice paper into warm water and place on the teatowel. They should be pliable and soft.

❉ Place some cold vermicelli, prawns, chicken, pork, pickled onion, pickles and carrot near the centre of the paper toward the bottom edge. Spread the filling out to a sausage shape.

❉ Roll the bottom edge of the rice paper up and tuck tightly under the mixture. Fold the left and right sides into the centre and then continue rolling away from you. This egg roll will be transparent and allow you to see the mixture inside. Continue until the mixture is used up. Refrigerate until ready to serve.

❉ Place the transparent egg rolls on a platter. Guests help themselves to lettuce leaves, one at a time. The roll is placed on the leaf and some mint and coriander are added. The whole is rolled up and dipped in the dipping sauce.

VIETNAMESE EGG ROLLS

SERVES 6	
100–125 g (4 oz) cellophane noodles	1 package of quadrant-shaped or round rice papers
2 dried Chinese mushrooms or 4 button mushrooms	vegetable oil for frying
2 pieces dried wood ears	**DIPPING SAUCE**
1 tbsp dried shrimp or 8 fresh prawns, finely chopped	2 tbsp nuoc mam sauce (page 72)
2 cloves garlic, ground	1 clove garlic, finely chopped
1 carrot, grated	1 red chilli pepper, finely chopped
1 onion, grated	2 tsp lime or lemon juice
110 g (4 oz) minced pork	1 tsp cider vinegar or wine vinegar
1 tbsp nuoc mam sauce (page 72), or 1 tbsp soy sauce with 2 anchovies crushed into it, and a dash of lime or lemon juice	1 tsp sugar
	TO SERVE
freshly ground black pepper	1 butterhead lettuce
1 egg, beaten	sprigs of coriander
	sprigs of mint

These delicious egg rolls should not be confused with the Chinese egg rolls. Traditionally, Vietnamese people would serve these at a party or a special occasion. They do take a bit of time to make and the rolling can sometimes be difficult to master, but the result is well worth the effort.

❉ First, make the dipping sauce. Combine all the ingredients in a dish and stir thoroughly.

❉ Soak the noodles in boiled water, slightly cooled, until soft and drain thoroughly. Cut with kitchen scissors to make shorter strands.

❉ Soak the Chinese mushrooms and wood ears in boiled water for 30 minutes. Squeeze them dry. Discard the stems and chop finely. If using button mushrooms, rinse, drain and chop finely.

❉ Soak the dried shrimp in boiled water that has cooled slightly until soft and then drain thoroughly; mince finely. If using fresh prawns, rinse, drain and mince.

❉ Place the noodles, garlic, carrot, onion, wood ears, mushrooms, dried shrimp, minced pork, nuoc mam sauce, black pepper and egg in a large mixing bowl. With your hands, mix all the ingredients thoroughly until the mixture is stiff enough to be shaped.

❉ Place some boiled water that has cooled slightly in a large bowl. Spread a clean teatowel on the surface you are going to roll on.

❉ If using square rice paper, take one piece and dip it into the water. Place it on the teatowel. Take another piece of rice paper and repeat. The rice paper should turn soft and pliable. (It is very important not to leave the rice paper too long in the water.)

❉ Place a second piece of rice paper on the first. The rounded edge of the quadrant should be at the bottom facing you and the second piece placed about 5 cm (2 in) above but overlapping. Place a small amount of the mixture where the pieces overlap at the bottom, on the rounded edge. Form the mixture into a sausage shape.

❉ Carefully roll the bottom rounded edge over the mixture, tucking the edge under the mixture. Fold over the left and right sides to the middle, then roll the egg roll away from you. Repeat these steps until all the mixture has been used. Be careful not to pack your rolls with too much mixture and try to roll them as tightly as possible, otherwise they will burst when fried.

❉ If using the round rice paper, pass it through the water and place it on the teatowel. Put some mixture roughly in the centre but closer to the edge nearest to you. Form the mixture into a sausage shape. Roll up as above. If one piece of round rice paper tears then use two, one on top of the other.

❉ When all the rolls are ready, heat the oil until hot in a large pan. Shallow fry the egg rolls, turning them frequently, until the mixture is cooked, taking care not to burn the rice paper. If you wish to deep-fry, put less filling in the rolls to ensure it is thoroughly cooked before the outside burns. Drain well on absorbent kitchen towels.

❉ Place the egg rolls in the center of a lettuce leaf, with some mint and coriander. Roll up and dip into the dipping sauce while still hot.

BEEF CRYSTAL EGG ROLLS

SERVES 4

225 g (8 oz) steak, cut against the grain into pieces 2.5 mm (⅛-in) thick and 5-cm (2-in) long

175 g (6 oz) rice vermicelli

2 pickled onions, finely sliced

2 dill pickles, finely sliced

1 carrot, grated

1 package round rice paper

warmed water in a bowl on the table

MARINADE

1 tsp finely crushed lemon grass (if this is unavailable, use the juice of a lemon and its grated zest)

1 tsp finely crushed garlic

1 tbsp ginger wine

DIPPING SAUCE

4 tbsp nuoc mam sauce (page 72)

1 red chilli pepper, finely chopped

1 clove garlic, finely chopped

1 tbsp lime or lemon juice

1 tsp wine vinegar

1 tsp sugar

2 tsp dry sherry

TO SERVE

1 butterhead lettuce

sprigs of coriander

Combine the marinade ingredients together and add the beef slices. Leave to marinate for 2 to 3 hours.

❀ Soak the rice vermicelli in boiled water, slightly cooled. When soft, drain thoroughly.

❀ Toss the cold rice vermicelli, pickled onion, dill pickles and carrot together and place on the table in a dish.

❀ Prepare the dipping sauce by mixing all the ingredients together and stir well.

❀ Put the lettuce leaves in a dish and the coriander and mint on a flat plate. Place the dish and plate on the table. Put the rice papers on a plate and place on the table.

❀ Put warm water in a bowl that is large enough for the rice papers to be dipped in on the table.

Put either a table-top barbecue or a fondue on the table and bring the marinated meat to the table for the guests to cook. If neither is available, grill the meat very quickly, or fry in a pan with a little vegetable oil, until tender. Either way the cooking time needs to be minimal, as thinly cut meat cooks extremely quickly; excessive cooking will toughen the meat.

❀ Guests should help themselves by dipping a rice paper into the warm water until it becomes soft and pliable. They then place some of the vermicelli and pickle, mint and coriander and the cooked pieces of beef on the rice paper. The mixture is then rolled up and placed on a fresh piece of lettuce. The lettuce leaf is rolled around it and then dipped in the sauce.

FRESH EGG ROLLS

SERVES 4 TO 6	
2 Chinese sweet sausages, combined weight about 100–125 g (4 oz)	225 g (8 oz) beansprouts, lightly blanched
200 g (7 oz) firm tofu	200 g (7 oz) spring onions
225 g (8 oz) crabmeat	**EGG ROLL SAUCE**
2 tbsp vegetable oil	225 ml (7 fl oz) chicken stock
2 eggs, beaten lightly	90 ml (6 tbsp) sugar
100–125 g (4 oz) cucumber	60 ml (4 tbsp) tamarind juice
8 to 12 egg roll wrappers or won tons	1 tbsp cornflour

Steam the Chinese sausages for about 8 minutes. Add the tofu and continue steaming for 3 minutes longer. Remove and cut both into pieces about the width of a pencil and about 10 cm (4 in) long.

❊ Steam the crabmeat for 5 minutes and set aside.

❊ Heat a nonstick shallow pan over medium heat. Add a drop of oil and just enough egg to cover the bottom—it should resemble a thin crêpe.

❊ Cook for 1 minute on each side. Make 8 to 12 thin omelettes in the same way. Roll them up and slice them into lengths the same size as the sausage and tofu.

❊ Cut the cucumber and spring onions into similar lengths too.

❊ Take each egg roll wrapper and lay it flat. Place on top 1 piece of tofu, sausage, cucumber and spring onion. Add 1 teaspoon of crab, several strips of egg and some beansprouts. Roll up carefully and cut each into 3 pieces.

❊ Place all the sauce ingredients, except the cornflour, in a pan and boil for 5 minutes. Mix the cornflour with a drop of water and add to the pan. Boil for 1 minute and take off the heat.

❊ Serve the egg rolls as they are or steam them for 1 to 2 minutes. Sprinkle with more crab to serve, 1 teaspoon of egg roll sauce, and extra chopped spring onion if liked. Serve the sauce alongside.

CRISPY "SEAWEED"

SERVES 4

675 to 750 g (1½ to 1¾ lb) cabbage or collard greens

600 ml (1 pt) vegetable oil for deep-frying

1 tsp salt

1 tsp sugar

You might be surprised to learn that the popular "seaweed" served in Chinese restaurants is, in fact, green cabbage! Choose fresh, young collards with pointed heads. Even the deep green outer leaves are quite tender. This recipe also makes an ideal garnish for a number of dishes, particularly cold appetizers and buffet dishes.

❀ Rinse and dry the cabbage or collard greens leaves and shred them with a sharp knife into the thinnest possible shavings. Spread them out on paper towels or put in a large colander to dry thoroughly.

❀ Heat the oil in a wok or deep-fat fryer. Before the oil gets too hot, turn off the heat for 30 seconds. Add the cabbage or collard greens shavings in several batches and turn the heat up to medium–high. Stir with a pair of cooking chopsticks.

❀ When the shavings start to float to the surface, scoop them out gently with a slotted spoon and drain them on absorbent kitchen paper to remove as much of the oil as possible. Sprinkle the salt and sugar evenly on top and mix gently. Serve at room temperature.

CHICKEN SATAY

SERVES 4

2 tbsp plain yoghurt

1 clove garlic, crushed

1 tsp chilli powder

1 tsp ground cumin

1 tsp ground coriander

1 tbsp lemon juice

335 g (12 oz) cubed uncooked
skinned chicken breast meat

DIPPING SAUCE

2 tbsp plain yoghurt

1 clove garlic, crushed

½ tsp ground cumin

1 tsp ground ginger

1 tsp ground coriander

1 tbsp lemon juice

1 tbsp chopped fresh mint

Combine the yoghurt with the garlic, chilli powder, cumin, coriander and lemon juice. Add the chicken pieces and marinate in the mixture in the refrigerator for at least 4 hours, turning frequently.

❋ Make the dipping sauce by mixing all the ingredients, except the mint, together. Leave to blend in a cool place.

❋ When the chicken is ready, thread it onto 4 skewers.

❋ Place on the barbecue or under a preheated high grill and cook until well done, basting frequently with the marinade and turning the skewers over.

❋ Heat the dipping sauce and toss in the mint leaves. Serve separately.

BEEF SATAY

SERVES 4

2 cloves garlic, crushed and
sliced

1 tsp fresh basil

1 red chilli pepper, sliced

1 tbsp lime juice

1 tbsp sesame oil

1 tbsp nuoc mam sauce
(page 72) (optional)

225 g (8 oz) steak, cubed

DIPPING SAUCE

3 tbsp nuoc mam sauce
(page 72)

1 tbsp lime or lemon juice

1 pickled onion, thinly sliced

1 clove garlic, finely chopped

1 tbsp peanuts, finely chopped

Mix the garlic, basil, chilli, lime juice, sesame oil and nuoc mam sauce, if using, together. Add the cubes of beef and marinate in the refrigerator for at least 4 hours, turning frequently.

❋ Make the dipping sauce by mixing all the ingredients together. Set aside until ready to serve, then place in a bowl on the table.

❋ When the beef is ready, thread onto 4 skewers.

❋ Place on the barbecue or under a preheated high grill until cooked, turning the skewers over frequently and basting with the reserved marinade.

PRAWN AND SCALLOP SATAY

150 ml (¼ pt) dry sherry or dry white wine

1 tbsp wine vinegar

1 tbsp chopped dill

salt to taste

12 large scallops, rinsed

12 large prawns in their shells

1 cucumber, cut into 1-cm (½-in) slices

SPICY TOMATO DIPPING SAUCE

1 large onion, finely chopped

2 tbsp vegetable oil

2 cloves garlic, chopped and crushed

2 fresh red chilli peppers, finely chopped

6 tomatoes, skinned

1 tbsp chopped sweet basil

Satay is bite-sized pieces of succulent meat, seafood, poultry or vegetables, seasoned and cooked over charcoal. A dipping sauce is always presented with the satay.

❉ Place the sherry, vinegar, dill and salt in a pan and bring to a boil. Reduce the heat to a simmer and add the scallops.

❉ Simmer for 2 minutes. Remove the scallops and reserve the liquid to use as the baste when barbecuing.

❉ Skewer the prawns, cucumber and scallops alternately so each skewer has 3 prawns, 3 scallops and 3 pieces of cucumber. Leave, covered, in a refrigerator.

❉ Gently fry the onions in the oil for 3 minutes. Add the garlic and fry for 1 minute.

❉ Add the chilli and tomatoes and fry for another 5 minutes. Add the basil leaves and stir. Remove from the heat and leave to cool.

❉ Place the skewers on the barbecue or under a preheated high grill and cook for 3 to 4 minutes on each side. Baste frequently with the reserved cooking liquid.

HOT-AND-SOUR
BEEF FONDUE

SERVES 4

300 ml (½ pt) good-quality beef stock

4 star anise

few cloves

few peppercorns

5-cm (2-in) piece fresh root ginger, peeled and chopped

1 onion, sliced

1 garlic clove, sliced

3 bird's-eye green chillies, seeded and sliced

3 tbsp red-wine vinegar

1 tbsp honey

350 g (12 oz) beef tenderloin, trimmed and sliced into thin strips

1 red pepper, seeded and cut into strips

1 yellow pepper, seeded and cut into strips

2 courgettes, trimmed and cut into strips

1 fresh pineapple, peeled, cored and cut into small wedges

175 g (6 oz) beansprouts

DIPPING SAUCE

1 tbsp soy sauce

2 tsp fish sauce

1 tsp honey, warmed

1 bird's-eye red chilli, seeded and sliced

This recipe is based on the Mongolian Hot Pot. The food is cooked in the hot stock which is then drunk at the end of the meal to clear the palate.

❀ Put the stock into a pan with the spices, ginger, onion, garlic and chillies. Bring to a boil, then lower the heat and simmer for 10 minutes. Add the vinegar and honey.

❀ Pour into a fondue pot placed over a burner and keep warm.

❀ Put the beef, peppers, courgettes and pineapple wedges into individual serving bowls.

❀ Combine the sauce ingredients and pour into small dishes.

❀ To serve, spear the beef or vegetables onto skewers. Dip each into the hot stock for 1 to 2 minutes, or until cooked to personal preference. Dip into the sauce before eating.

❀ When all the beef, vegetables and fruit have been eaten, add the beansprouts to the fondue pot and heat through for 1 to 2 minutes. Ladle into soup bowls and drink to clear the palate.

CHICKEN STRIPS WITH NUOC CHAM

SERVES 4

275 g (10 oz) boneless chicken breast, skinned

MARINADE

2 shallots, finely chopped

1 garlic clove, crushed

4 bird's-eye red chillies, seeded and chopped

5-cm (2-in) piece fresh root ginger, peeled and grated

2 tbsp soy sauce

2 tsp honey, warmed

2 tbsp lemon juice

chopped chilli, to garnish

NUOC CHAM

1 bird's-eye red chilli, seeded and finely chopped

1 tbsp lime juice

60 ml (4 tbsp) Thai fish sauce

1 tbsp roasted peanuts, finely crushed

2 spring onions, trimmed and finely shredded

Nuoc cham is a traditional Vietnamese dipping sauce served at the table to season dishes. The sauce can also be stirred into soups and rice dishes, or poured over fish and meat dishes.

❀ Cut the chicken breasts into narrow strips, about 7.5 x 1 cm (3 x ½ in), and place in a shallow dish. Combine all the marinade ingredients and pour over the chicken strips.

❀ Stir to ensure they are well coated.

❀ Cover the dish and chill for at least 3 hours, stirring the chicken occasionally in the marinade.

❀ If you are using wooden skewers, soak them in cold water for at least 1 hour before you plan to cook.

❀ Preheat the grill to medium-high.

❀ Drain the chicken and thread onto skewers.

❀ Meanwhile, prepare the nuoc cham sauce. Put all the ingredients into a small pan and heat through, stirring occasionally; set aside.

❀ Brush the chicken strips with a little of the marinade and grill, brushing occasionally with the marinade and turning the strips, for 8 to 10 minutes, or until tender and the juices run clear.

❀ Serve with the sauce, garnished with the chopped chilli.

Chicken Strips
with Nuoc Cham

CUCUMBER SALAD WITH CHILLIES

SERVES 4

1 large cucumber, peeled

1 small red onion, thinly sliced

2 or 3 red chillies, seeded and thinly sliced

2 tbsp lime juice

1 tbsp Thai fish sauce

2 tsp honey, warmed

1 tbsp sesame oil

rocket leaves

90 ml (6 tbsp) shelled large roasted peanuts, roughly chopped

The dressing for this salad is traditionally made with dried shrimp. If using, grind 2 tablespoons of shrimp to a fine powder in a mortar and pestle, then add to the dressing and pour over the cucumbers.

❀ Cut the cucumber in half lengthwise and cut into half-moon shapes. Place in a large shallow dish. Scatter the onion and chilli slices over.

❀ Mix together the lime juice, fish sauce, honey and oil. Pour over the cucumber and leave in a cool place for at least 30 minutes to let the flavours develop.

❀ Arrange the rocket leaves on a serving platter, top with the cucumber mixture and sprinkle with the peanuts.

MINCED PORK, CRAB AND GRAPEFRUIT SALAD

SERVES 4

175 g (6 oz) minced pork or beef

3 tbsp water

2 tbsp lime or lemon juice

2 tbsp nuoc mam sauce (page 72)

1 green chilli, finely sliced

1 small onion, finely diced

1-cm (½-in) piece fresh root ginger, peeled and finely chopped

1 tbsp finely chopped fresh coriander

1 small tin crabmeat, thoroughly drained

1 pink grapefruit, segmented and halved

GARNISH

lettuce leaves

grated carrot

Place the minced pork in the water and slowly cook over medium heat until the meat turns colour and is just cooked but still tender. Remove from the heat and leave to cool slightly.

✿ Add the lime juice, nuoc mam sauce and chilli to the meat. When thoroughly cooled, add the onion, ginger, coriander and crabmeat and stir together. Toss the grapefruit into the salad.

✿ Place the lettuce leaves on a flat dish. Arrange the grated carrot on the lettuce to form a ring. Spoon the salad into the centre of the carrot. Serve at once.

VIETNAMESE SALAD

SERVES 4

2 stalks fresh lemon grass
(discard outer leaves), thinly
sliced

225 g (8 oz) finely shredded
leftover roast beef, pork,
lamb, or chicken

1 bunch spring onions, washed
and finely chopped

2 carrots, finely grated

1 red chilli, finely sliced

2 cloves garlic, finely sliced
and crushed

3 tbsp nuoc mam sauce
(page 72)

½ cup lime or lemon juice

2 tbsp chopped fresh basil

2 tbsp finely chopped fresh
coriander

Most meals in Vietnam are accompanied by a salad or salad ingredients. Salads are also eaten as first courses or a side dish. A Vietnamese salad is never plain—Vietnamese are adventurous in their mixing of textures and tastes.

❀ Lightly hit the sliced lemon grass with the back of a cleaver or heavy knife to release the flavour and aroma.

❀ Mix the lemon grass with the leftover meat, then add the spring onions and toss together. Mix in the grated carrot.

❀ Mix together the chilli, garlic, nuoc mam sauce and lime juice and stir well. Add to the salad and toss well.

❀ Throw in the basil and coriander and toss again. If you think you need more salad dressing, add equal parts of nuoc mam sauce and lime

SIMPLE SALAD

SERVES 4

1 lettuce, finely shredded

1 cucumber, peeled and cut
lengthwise into thin strips

2 carrots, peeled and cut
lengthwise into thin strips

1 large handful of beansprouts,
rinsed and drained thoroughly

3 tbsp chopped fresh coriander

3 tbsp chopped fresh mint

2 hard-boiled eggs, quartered,
to garnish

SALAD DRESSING

4 tbsp nuoc mam sauce
(page 72)

4 tbsp lemon juice

1 tbsp wine vinegar

3 cloves garlic, crushed

1 tsp sugar

1 red chilli, finely chopped

3 tbsp crushed roasted peanuts

Combine the lettuce, cucumber, carrots and beansprouts. Stir lightly together.

❀ Mix the nuoc mam sauce, lemon juice and vinegar. Add the garlic and sugar and stir thoroughly, then add the chilli and peanuts and stir again.

❀ Toss the dressing into the salad and scatter the coriander and mint over the top. Garnish with the egg quarters.

SPICY SEAFOOD SALAD

SERVES 6

150 g (5 oz) sea bass or perch, cleaned, gutted and thinly sliced

150 g (5 oz) large raw prawns, shelled

150 g (5 oz) squid, body and tentacles, cleaned, gutted, and sliced into 1.5-cm (¾-in) strips

7 fresh bird's-eye green chillies

5 garlic cloves

2 coriander roots

2 tbsp fish sauce

½ tsp sugar

2 tbsp lime or lemon juice

4 spring onions, sliced

1 medium onion, thinly sliced

1 medium celery stick and leaves, sliced

The Thai versions of salad, of which this is one, are flavourful assemblies of different ingredients quite unlike those typically used in the West. Most are extremely spicy. This combines three of the basic five flavours: spicy, sour and salty.

❀ Cook the fish, prawns, and squid separately in salted water for 2 to 3 minutes each until tender and the prawns turn pink. Drain well.

❀ Pound the chillies, garlic, coriander root, fish sauce and sugar together with a mortar and pestle or in a blender until fine.

❀ Place the pounded ingredients in a bowl and mix in the lemon juice, spring onion, onion and celery. Stir in the seafood and mix well. Serve immediately.

MEAT SALAD WITH GRAPEFRUIT, MINT AND LEMON GRASS

SERVES 4

1 tbsp unsalted peanuts

1 tbsp sesame seeds

25 g (1 oz) dried shrimp, soaked in hot water for 30 minutes

50 g (2 oz) fresh pork

50 g (2 oz) raw prawns in the shells

salt

1 cucumber, unpeeled, halved lengthwise, seeded and sliced thinly

1 large carrot, shredded

110 g (4 oz) fresh beansprouts

25 g (1 oz) cooked chicken meat, cut into thin strips

1 tbsp chopped mint

½ tbsp chopped lemon grass

1 large grapefruit, peeled, sectioned and cut crosswise into 2-cm (1-in) pieces

coriander sprigs to garnish

EGG CREPES

2 eggs

¼ tsp nuoc mam sauce (page 72)

freshly ground black pepper

vegetable oil

DRESSING

1 clove garlic, crushed

1 fresh red chilli, seeded and minced

½ tbsp sugar

½ tbsp fresh lime juice

½ tbsp rice vinegar

1½ tbsp nuoc mam sauce (page 72)

Toast the peanuts in a hot, dry wok or nonstick pan, stirring constantly, for about 5 minutes until golden brown. Crush with a grinder or put between a couple of sheets of clean strong paper and crush with a rolling pin or milk bottle.

❀ Pour in half of the egg mixture and tilt the pan immediately to spread the mixture evenly over the bottom—the crêpe should be paper-thin. Cook until the egg is set—this should not take more than 30 seconds. Turn and cook on the other side for about 15 seconds. Set aside. Repeat, using up the rest of the mixture and set aside.

❀ Combine the garlic, chilli, sugar, lime juice, vinegar and nuoc mam sauce in a bowl and stir together; set aside.

❀ Drain the dried shrimp and pound until very fine; set aside.

❀ Place the pork in a saucepan, cover with water, and bring to a boil. Lower the heat and simmer for about 30 minutes, or until the juices run clear when the meat is pierced with a knife. Run cold water over the pork and set aside.

❀ Cook the raw prawns in boiling water for about 2 minutes until it is just pink. Run cold water over them, then drain, shell, de-vein and cut lengthwise in halves. Shred the prawns and set aside.

❀ Sprinkle salt over the cucumber and carrot, and leave to stand for 15 minutes. Run cold water over them and squeeze dry with your hands. It is imperative that the vegetables are bone dry to ensure their crunchiness.

❀ Dip the beansprouts in salted boiling water for 30 seconds. Run cold water over them and drain.

❀ Cut the egg crêpes into thin strips.

❀ Combine the egg crêpe strips, dried shrimp, shredded prawn, chicken, cucumber, carrot, beansprouts, mint, lemon grass, grapefruit and sesame seeds. Mix well with your hands. Pour the dressing over.

❀ Transfer to a serving dish or serve separately, and sprinkle the crushed peanuts over it. Garnish with coriander. Alternatively, serve in hollowed grapefruit shells instead of a serving dish.

❀ Toast the sesame seeds in the same way for only 3 minutes. Grind lightly to a grainy texture.

❀ To make the thin egg crêpes, beat the eggs, nuoc mam sauce and pepper together with ½ teaspoon water in a bowl. Brush the bottom of a nonstick omelette pan with some oil and place over medium heat until hot.

SEAFOOD DISHES

STEAMED FISH WITH LEMON AND CHILLI

SERVES 4

500 g (1 lb 2 oz) whole sea bass or sea perch, cleaned and gutted

125 ml (4 fl oz) lemon or lime juice

2 tbsp lightly chopped fresh small green chillies

2 tbsp chopped garlic

2 tbsp fish sauce

½ tbsp salt

1 tsp sugar

60 ml (4 tbsp) coriander leaves and stems cut into 1-cm (½-in) pieces

freshly cooked rice to serve

Steam the fish whole for 15 minutes until it is tender but still firm.

✿ Meanwhile, mix all the remaining ingredients, except the coriander, together.

✿ When the fish is cooked, place it on a serving platter and spread the lemon juice mixture all over; the fish must be very hot when the sauce is poured over.

✿ Sprinkle with the coriander and serve accompanied by rice.

SCALLOPS STUFFED WITH SHRIMP PASTE

SERVES 4

12 scallops, cleaned

vegetable oil for frying

SHRIMP PASTE STUFFING

1 tbsp dried shrimp, soaked in water until soft, drained, and finely chopped, or 20 defrosted frozen shrimps, finely chopped

2 small pieces of dried wood ears, soaked in warm water until soft, drained, and finely chopped

225 g (8 oz) mashed sweet potato

1 tbsp nuoc mam sauce (page 72), or 1 tbsp soy sauce

Make the shrimp paste stuffing by combining all the ingredients together.

❁ Steam the scallops for about 5 minutes until tender and cooked through; remove and leave to cool.

❁ Slit the scallops in their thickest part and spoon in the stuffing.

❁ Heat the oil in a wok or heavy-bottomed saucepan until very hot. Gently lower the stuffed scallops in a basket and deep-fry for 2 minutes.

PRAWNS FRIED WITH GARLIC AND PEPPER

SERVES 4

about 125 ml (6 fl oz) vegetable oil for frying

300 g (11 oz) raw large prawns, shelled

½ tbsp lightly chopped garlic

2 tbsp ground white pepper

1 tsp salt

freshly cooked rice and thin cucumber slices to serve

Heat the oil in a wok or large pan until smoking. Add the shrimp and stir-fry until lightly browned.

❀ Remove all but 2 tablespoons of the oil. Add the garlic, pepper and salt to the shrimp in the pan. Fry lightly for 2 minutes longer until brown.

❀ Drain off most of the remaining oil and serve immediately accompanied by rice and sliced cucumber.

PRAWNS WITH COCONUT MILK AND CHILLI PASTE

SERVES 4

450 ml (¾ pt) thin coconut milk

450 g (1 lb) raw large prawns

2 tbsp fish sauce

1½ tbsp sugar

2 fresh large red chillies, cut into matchsticks

1 tbsp coriander leaves

1 tsp shredded kaffir lime leaf

CHILLI PASTE

5 dried red chillies, roughly chopped

1½ tbsp sliced shallot

½ tbsp finely sliced lemon grass

½ tbsp chopped garlic

2 tsp salt

1 tsp shrimp paste

1 tsp sliced galangal

½ tsp chopped kaffir lime peel

½ tsp chopped coriander root or stem

Pound all the ingredients for the chilli paste together with a mortar and pestle or in a blender to form a fine paste.

❀ Heat 225 ml (7 fl oz) of the coconut milk in a wok or large saucepan. Add the chilli paste and simmer for 2 to 3 minutes until fragrant.

❀ Add the prawns and fry for 1 minute, then add the rest of the coconut milk, the fish sauce, and sugar. Boil for 2 minutes, then remove from the heat. Transfer to a serving bowl and garnish with the coriander, chilli and lime leaf. Serve accompanied by rice.

SOUR CURRY SOUP

SERVES 4

425 g (15 oz) whole freshwater
fish, cleaned and gutted

1.25 l (2 pt) water

½ cucumber, quartered
and sliced lengthwise

110 g (4 oz) green beans, cut
into 5-cm (2-in) pieces

225 g (8 oz) morning glory or
swamp cabbage cut into
5-cm (2-in) pieces

225 g (8 oz) Chinese cabbage
cut into 5-cm (2-in) pieces

3 tbsp tamarind juice

2 tbsp fish sauce

2 tsp lemon juice

1 tsp sugar

CHILI PASTE

8 dried red chillies, chopped

3 chopped shallots

1 tbsp chopped krachai

1 tbsp salt

½ tsp shrimp paste

A delicious soup with lots of vegetables. The bones are cooked with the fish for more flavour. Serve accompanied by rice, sun-dried beef or dry salted fish, and pickled vegetables as condiments.

❁ Cut the fish into 3 cm (1½ in) long pieces. Boil 150 g (5 oz) of it in water until cooked, then remove with a slotted spoon (discard the water) and leave to cool. Remove all the bones, but retain the skin.

❁ Pound all the ingredients for the chilli paste together with a mortar and pestle or in a blender. Mix in the cooked fish pieces and pound or process again.

❁ Place the fish-chilli paste in a wok or large pan large enough to hold all the ingredients. Add the water and bring to a boil.

❁ Add the rest of the fish and boil again for 2 minutes, then add the cucumber, beans, morning glory and Chinese cabbage. Return to a boil, add the rest of the ingredients, and simmer for 10

STUFFED CRAB

SERVES 4

2 cooked crabs

110 g (4 oz) chopped lean pork

1 onion, chopped

1 tsp black pepper

1 tbsp sugar

1 tbsp nuoc mam sauce (page 72)

1 tbsp chopped coriander root

2 eggs, separated

1 tbsp chopped spring onions

1 tbsp chopped fresh coriander leaves

1 fresh red or green chilli, finely sliced

Remove the limbs from the crabs. Remove the flesh from the shells, taking care to keep them intact. Remove the flesh from the limbs as well. Flake all the flesh and set aside.

❋ Combine the pork, onion, pepper, sugar, nuoc mam sauce, and cilantro root in a blender.

❋ Add the crabmeat and egg white. Add the spring onions and coriander leaves and mix by hand, using more egg white if necessary.

❋ Fill the crab shells with the mixture to form a generous mound. Carefully break the egg yolk and place ½ teaspoon yolk on the top of each mound. Sprinkle with chilli. Be very careful when moving the crab shells or else the yolk will run; if you think this is too difficult, brush the filling with the beaten egg yolk and sprinkle with the sliced chilli and some coriander leaves.

❋ Place each crab, stuffed side up, in a large steamer. Steam for 20 minutes. Serve with a generous green salad.

STIR-FRIED SEAFOOD WITH MINT, GARLIC AND CHILLIES

SERVES 4

100–125 g (4 oz) fish fillets

6 mussels

1 small uncooked crab, cleaned and chopped

100–125 g (4 oz) squid pieces

100–125 g (4 oz) prawns

100–125 g (4 oz) scallops

2 cloves garlic, chopped

2 large fresh chillies, chopped

1 tbsp chopped coriander roots

1 tbsp vegetable oil

2 tbsp oyster sauce

2 tbsp nuoc mam sauce (page 72)

1 red pepper, seeded and cut in strips

1 onion, thinly sliced

2 shallots, thinly sliced

4 tbsp chopped fresh mint

freshly cooked rice to serve

herbs to garnish

Rinse and prepare the seafood. Cut the fish fillets into bite-sized pieces. Scrub the mussels and remove the beards.

❋ Take the limbs off the crab and crack the shell with a hammer so the meat is easy to remove at the table. Remove the outer shell, clean out the crab body, and break into bite-sized pieces.

❋ Put the garlic, chillies and coriander root in a blender and make a coarse paste; set aside.

❋ Heat the oil in a wok or large pan over medium heat. Add the garlic, chilli and coriander. Add the seafood and stir-fry gently so the fish fillet does not break up. Add the oyster sauce and nuoc mam sauce. Taste, cover and simmer for a few minutes.

❋ Remove the lid and add the pepper, onion, shallots and mint, and stir-fry gently (the fish fillets are now even more delicate) for a couple of minutes.

❋ Arrange the seafood on a large, shallow serving dish. Garnish with whatever herbs you happen to have. Serve with a large bowl of steaming rice.

FRIED FISH TOPPED WITH CHILLI SAUCE

8 garlic cloves

5 fresh yellow chillies

1 kg (2¼ lb) whole perch or sea bass, cleaned and gutted

about 750 ml (1¼ pt) vegetable oil for frying

½ tsp each salt and freshly ground white pepper

flour for dusting

125 ml (4 fl oz) chicken stock

2 fresh chillies, quartered lengthwise

1 tbsp tamarind juice or vinegar

2 tsp sugar

1 tsp fish sauce

110 g (2 oz) sweet basil leaves, fried in oil for 1 minute until crisp and well drained

freshly cooked rice to serve

The scoring makes small trenches in the flesh for the sauce, which is not intended to surround the fish, but to be poured on top at the last minute.

❁ Pound the garlic and chilli together lightly with a mortar and pestle or in a blender.

❁ Score the fish on both sides 5 or 6 times, then sprinkle with the salt and pepper and dust with flour.

❁ Heat the oil to 180°C/350°F in a wok or large pan. Add the fish and fry for 7 to 10 minutes until crisp but tender. Remove and drain the fish well. Put it in a serving dish.

❁ Take out all except about 60 ml (4 tbsp) of the oil. Add the garlic and chilli mixture and stir-fry.

❁ Add the rest of the ingredients, except for the basil, and boil lightly for about 5 minutes until slightly thick. Pour on top of the fish and sprinkle the fried basil over to garnish. Serve accompanied by rice.

MACKEREL COOKED IN POT LINED WITH PORK

SERVES 4

2 large mackerel, cleaned

2 cakes tofu

salt and freshly ground black pepper

3 tbsp vegetable oil

100–125 g (4 oz) fresh pork, cut into threads

100–125 g (4 oz) dried Chinese mushrooms, soaked in warm water for 30 minutes, drained and cut into threads

110 g (4 oz) sliced bamboo shoots

1 red chilli, chopped

2 slices fresh root ginger, chopped

1 tbsp soy sauce

1 tbsp nuoc mam sauce (page 72)

½ tbsp wine

600 ml (1 pt) water

2 spring onions, chopped

Chop the mackerel into slices about 2 cm (1 in) thick.

❀ Rinse the tofu, then salt lightly to absorb the water. Season. Cut the bean curds in half and then cut them into cubes.

❀ Heat 1 tablespoon of the oil in a wok or large pan. Add the tofu cubes and stir-fry; set aside.

❀ Add 1 tablespoon oil to the wok and fry the mackerel until both sides turn golden brown. Add the remaining oil.

❀ Add the pork, black mushrooms, bamboo shoots, chilli, root ginger, soy sauce, nuoc mam sauce, wine and sugar and stir-fry.

❀ Pour the contents of the wok into a flameproof casserole. Add the water and bring to a boil over high heat. Lower the heat to low and braise the fish for 20 minutes.

❀ Taste and add the spring onions. Serve hot.

LOBSTER AND SWEET POTATO CURRY

SERVES 4	
25 g (1 oz) unsalted butter	1 dried chilli, seeds removed, crushed
450 g (1 lb) sweet potatoes, peeled and cut into 2-cm (1-in) cubes	2 tsp cumin seeds
	1 tbsp coriander seeds
1 tbsp sake or dry sherry	1 tsp dried lemon grass, sliced
1 whole lobster, chopped into 2-cm (1-in) cubes	1 tsp ground galangal
	2 tsp grated lemon zest
	2 tbsp chopped fresh coriander
CURRY SAUCE	1 tsp salt
1 tbsp vegetable oil	1 tsp ground turmeric
1 medium onion, chopped	2 tsp sweet paprika
1 tbsp crushed garlic	
2 tsp shrimp paste	

Make the curry sauce by heating the oil in a wok or large pan over medium-high heat. Add the onion and garlic and stir-fry for 5 minutes or until soft. Add the shrimp paste and stir thoroughly, pressing the paste to blend it well. Cook for 3 or so minutes longer, then remove from the heat.

❃ Grind the chilli, cumin seeds, coriander seeds, and lemon grass together with a mortar and pestle or in a blender until powdery.

❃ Place the onion mixture in a blender or food processor and blend until very smooth. Add the ground spices, galangal, lemon zest, fresh coriander, salt, turmeric and paprika. Blend until the mixture becomes a smooth paste; this makes about 60 ml curry sauce.

❃ Wipe out the wok or pan. Add the butter and melt. Add the sweet potatoes and cook for 15 minutes, taking care the potatoes do not burn.

❃ Stir in the curry sauce and sake until the curry mixture is dissolved. Add the lobster cubes and cook for 2 to 3 minutes longer.

SUSHI

RAINBOW ROLL

*1 unsliced California Roll
(page 91)*

*paper-thin slices raw fish
(see introduction)*

*paper-thin slices avocado,
brushed with lemon juice*

*black sesame seeds to garnish
(optional)*

One of the most colourful inside-out rolls, easily made by adding a garnish of paper-thin avocado and raw fish to a California Roll (page 91). Take care when you select the fish because the colour of the type you use will determine the overall look of this piece of sushi. Use white halibut, creamy coloured yellowtail, rosy orange smoked salmon or red bonita. For a striking appearance, the fish must be very thin but still thick enough to show some colour.

❀ Prepare the California Roll as on page 91 but do not slice it.

❀ Place strips of raw fish and avocado on top of the California Roll, arranging them so you have a contrast of colours. Sprinkling with black sesame seeds creates a dramatic effect.

❀ Place a piece of clingfilm over the seaweed-paper roll. Then place the roll on a bamboo sushi rolling mat and re-roll the seaweed-paper roll so it becomes tight and compressed.

❀ Unwrap the seaweed-paper roll. Carefully cut the roll into 6 equal pieces. If you are not experienced at slicing delicate sushi, it is easier to cut it while it is still rolled in clingfilm.

CALIFORNIA ROLL

MAKES 6 PIECES

1 sheet nori

small portion sushi rice (page 28)

sesame seeds

wasabi

thinly sliced strips of cucumber and avocado

crabmeat, thawed and well drained if frozen

red fish roe to garnish (optional)

This is an example of a type of sushi known as an inside-out roll, and as the name suggests, California Roll is hardly a classical sushi recipe. It is, however, extremely popular on the West coast of the United States, and has even made the menu of Tokyo sushi bars. It is a superb blend of textures: cooked crab, avocado and cucumber. And, of course it appeals to people who want to try sushi but are uncomfortable about eating raw fish.

❀ Place the nori on a bamboo sushi rolling mat. Spread the top with a thin layer of sushi rice and sprinkle with sesame seeds. Press down gently so the rice sticks to the nori.

❀ Very gently turn the nori over so the rice is on the bottom.

❀ Arrange the cucumber and avocado strips along the length of the nori in the middle.

❀ Place the crabmeat over the top of the cucumber and avocado strips.

❀ Starting from the long end closest to you, roll up the nori jelly-roll fashion.

❀ Place a piece of clingfilm over the nori roll. Then place the roll on a bamboo sushi rolling mat and re-roll the nori roll so it becomes tight and compressed.

❀ Unwrap the nori roll. Sprinkle the fish roe along the top to add colour if you like. Carefully cut the roll into 6 equal pieces.

❀ To serve, arrange the pieces on a plate in 2 rows next to each other, with the end pieces in the middle.

SPICY TUNA SUSHI

MAKES 6 PIECES

soy sauce

hot-pepper paste

fresh tuna cut into 5-mm (¼-in) strips

very finely chopped green part of a spring onion

1 sheet seaweed paper

small portion sushi rice (page 28)

sesame seeds (optional)

With spicy sushi, it is best to use strong-flavoured fish, such as tuna, as in this recipe, or bonita, yellowtail or even shark. Otherwise, the flavour of the fish is overwhelmed by the spices. If you include sesame oil in your ingredients, however, do not use the fatty belly cuts of fish because the result will be greasy.

This recipe includes finely chopped spring onions, but you can use chopped daikon sprouts instead.

❁ Mix the soy sauce and hot-pepper paste together, adjusting the amount of hot-pepper sauce to taste; you need just enough to cover the tuna strips. Add the tuna and spring onion and gently stir so the tuna will be coated with the mixture on all sides. Set aside to marinate.

❁ Place the seaweed paper on a bamboo sushi rolling mat. Spread it with a thin layer of sushi rice and sprinkle with sesame seeds if you want.

Press down gently so the rice sticks to the paper.

❁ Very gently turn the seaweed paper over so the rice is on the bottom.

❁ Arrange the tuna strips along the length of the seaweed paper in the middle. You can sprinkle with the spring onion slices from the marinade if you like, or discard them.

❁ Starting from the long end closest to you, roll up the seaweed paper, jelly-roll fashion, so the rice is on the outside.

❁ Place a piece of clingfilm over the seaweed-paper roll. Then place the roll on a bamboo sushi rolling mat and re-roll the seaweed-paper roll so it becomes tight and compressed.

❁ Unwrap the seaweed-paper roll. Carefully cut the roll into 6 equal pieces. If you are not experienced at cutting delicate sushi, it is easier to cut it while it is still rolled in clingfilm.

DEEP-FRIED TOFU

MAKES 8 PIECES

4 deep-fried tofu pouches

*small portion sushi rice
(page 28)*

sesame seeds (optional)

*pickled ginger, well drained
and finely chopped (optional)*

BRAISING STOCK

125 ml (4 fl oz) dashi (page 27)

100–125 g (4 oz) sugar

3 tbsp soy sauce

2 tbsp sake

Called inari in Japanese, these are stuffed deep-fried tofu pouches that are braised just before serving. They are quick and easy to make because the tofu pouches are bought already deep-fried from Oriental grocery stores. You will find the pouches frozen in a freezer or fresh ones in the chill cabinet; if they are not frozen, they should be used within four days. The braising stock can also be made in advance and refrigerated for up to a week.

The blandness of these makes them something of an acquired taste, but they are economical, keep well, and are an ideal project for anyone new to sushi making.

❀ Blanch the tofu pouches in boiling water for a few seconds to remove any excess oil. Drain well and pat dry with absorbent kitchen paper.

❀ While the tofu pouches are still warm, cut them in half. To create the pockets for stuffing, place a half-pouch in the palm of one hand and slap it quite smartly with the other hand. This will loosen it in the middle so you can open it up to form the pocket.

❀ Place a small amount of sushi rice inside each pouch, pressing it in with your thumb. Add a small amount of sesame seed and pickled ginger if you want extra texture and flavour.

❀ Carefully close the pouch, tucking one flap inside and the other onto the bottom.

❀ To make the braising stock, place all the ingredients in a pan and stir until the sugar dissolves. Add the stuffed pouches and simmer them for 6 to 7 minutes, basting frequently with the stock. Turn off the heat and leave the pouches to cool in the liquid.

❀ When the liquid is cool, remove the pouches from the pan and drain well on absorbent kitchen paper. Serve at once, or chill until required.

SALMON SKIN TEMAKI

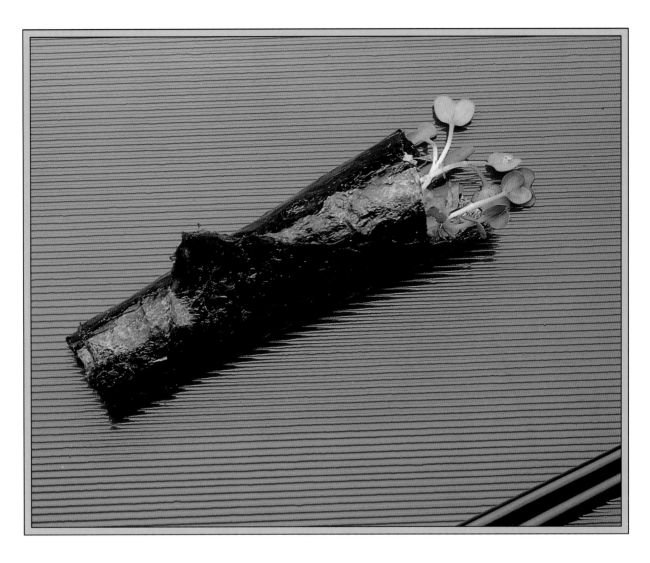

MAKES 1 PIECE

2-cm (1-in) wide strip of
salmon with its skin

½ strip of nori, cut
horizontally

small portion of sushi rice

*fine, thin strips of cucumber
and carrot*

sprigs of garden cress

Temaki are a relatively recent innovation in
sushi. They are loose, hand-rolled pieces of
nori assembled without the aid of a rolling mat.
You can use almost any ingredient for the filling,
such as salad ingredients, marinades and sauce,
fish, meat and soft and semi-liquid ingredients,
such as roe or sea urchin. If you do use a soft
filling, however, you will find it easier to roll nori
into a cone with the rice in the bottom and the
extra ingredient on top.

❀ Preheat the grill. Place the strip of salmon on a
piece of foil, skin side up, and place under the
grill just until it is cooked through and the skin
flakes easily.

❀ Slice the grilled salmon into several thinner
strips.

❀ Spread the rice over the nori from one end to
the middle. Add the salmon and vegetables in a
bunch, positioning them so they overlap the top
slightly.

❀ Roll the nori around the filling ingredients, so
the end with the ingredients over the edge is
slightly wider than the other end.

TIGER EYE

MAKES 4 SLICES

raw squid fillet, about 1-cm (½-in) thick

½ sheet nori, cut into a square

smoked salmon

white fish cake

1 cooked jumbo prawn, shelled and butterflied

This is an example of the fancy sushi itamae, sushi master chefs, make to prove their virtuosity. It requires time, patience and dexterity to make.

❀ Place the squid fillet horizontally on a chopping board in front of you. With the blade of a filleting knife held flat, slice the fillet horizontally through the thickness, from left to right, without cutting through the left or right side. This will form a tube in the middle of the squid. Set aside until required.

❀ Preheat the grill.

❀ Place the nori on the countertop in front of you and cover half of it with smoked salmon. The salmon should go to the edge but no further.

❀ Place a strip of white fish cake in the middle of the smoked salmon. Place the prawn on top of this. Lay more smoked salmon on top.

❀ Roll up the nori, enclosing the above ingredients. Trim off any excess if the roll is too thick to fit into the squid tube.

❀ Gently slide the nori roll in the squid tube.

❀ Place the stuffed squid under the grill for a few minutes. This will cook the squid so it contracts around the nori roll.

❀ To serve, slice the squid roll into 4 equal pieces.

EGG OMELETTE

MAKES 8 BLOCKS OF OMELETS

60 ml (4 tbsp) dashi (page 27)
75 g (3 oz) sugar
1½ tsp soy sauce
1½ tsp sake
½ tsp salt
5 eggs
vegetable oil

This sweetened egg omelette is traditionally eaten at the end of sushi meal as a dessert. It is made in a rectangular omelette pan, which is sold in Oriental grocery stores. For an unsweetened version, often included in mixed sushi, omit the sugar.

❀ Combine the dashi, sugar, soy sauce, sake and salt in a bowl and stir until the sugar and salt dissolve. If the dashi is still hot, let the mixture cool to room temperature.

❀ Beat the eggs, introducing as little air as possible; you do not want a fluffy mixture.

❀ Add the cool liquid to the eggs.

❀ Lightly grease the pan with the vegetable oil. Pour about one-quarter of the mixture into the pan, tilting the pan so the bottom is evenly and thinly coated.

❀ Cook over medium heat until the eggs are barely set, pricking any bubbles with a long chopstick. This is where the difference from a Western omelette starts to become obvious.

❀ Use chopsticks to fold the omelette in half, folding the omelette from the front of the pan back toward the end with the handle. Leave the front half of the pan empty.

❀ Lightly oil the empty part of the pan by putting some vegetable oil on a crumpled piece of absorbent kitchen paper and using the chopsticks to move the paper around the pan.

❀ Slide the omelette down to the oiled part of the pan.

❀ Pour one-third of the remaining batter into the pan. Use the chopsticks to lift the cooked omelette so the uncooked batter runs underneath.

❀ Continue cooking the omelette until the eggs are barely set. Use the chopsticks to fold the omelette down to handle-end of the pan and repeat the process until all the egg mixture is used.

❀ Cook the final block of omelette a little longer than in the previous steps to caramelize the sugar on the surface. Invert it onto a flat surface to cool.

❀ When cool, cut the thick omelette into 8 strips. To serve, garnish with finely grated daikon or wrap thin strips of nori around each piece.

POULTRY DISHES

CHICKEN FRIED WITH GREEN PEPPER

<table>
<tr><td colspan="2" align="center">SERVES 4</td></tr>
</table>

1 medium vegetable oil	1 medium onion, thickly sliced
1 tbsp chopped garlic	1 tbsp oyster sauce
300 g (11 oz) boneless skinned chicken breasts, cut lengthwise into 1-cm (½-in) slices	¾ tbsp soy sauce
	1 tsp fish sauce
	110 g (4 oz) sweet basil leaves
1 large sliced green pepper	freshly cooked rice to serve
5 fresh red chillies, sliced lengthwise	

Heat the oil in a wok or large pan until smoking. Add the garlic and chicken and stir-fry for 1 minute.

❀ Add the green pepper and chilli, mix, then add the onion and cook for 1 minute.

❀ One by one, stir in the rest of the ingredients, stir-frying for about 30 seconds after each addition. Remove from the heat immediately after stirring in the basil. Serve accompanied by rice.

CHICKEN FRIED WITH BASIL

SERVES 4

8 fresh green chillies, lightly chopped

8 garlic cloves, lightly chopped

60 ml (4 tbsp) vegetable oil

300 g (11 oz) boneless skinned minced chicken

2 fresh red chillies, quartered lengthwise

1 tbsp oyster sauce

½ tsp fish sauce

¼ tsp soy sauce

90 ml (6 tbsp) sweet basil leaves

freshly cooked rice to serve

Pound the green chilli and garlic together with a mortar and pestle or in a blender.

❁ Heat the oil in a wok or large pan until smoking. Add the chilli-garlic mixture and stir-fry for 1 minute

❁ Add the chicken and stir-fry for 1 minute, then add the red chilli, oyster sauce, fish sauce and soy sauce. Stir-fry for 2 minutes.

❁ Stir in the basil and serve immediately accompanied by rice.

SWEET-AND-SOUR CHICKEN

900 ml (1½ pt) vegetable oil

425 g (15 oz) boneless skinned chicken breasts, cut across into 5-mm (¼-in) slices

flour for coating

1 onion, sliced

1 green pepper, seeded and sliced

125 ml (4 fl oz) tomato ketchup

125 ml (4 fl oz) tomato quarters

110 g (4 oz) diced pineapple

125 ml (4 fl oz) chicken stock

2 tsp soy sauce

1 tsp sugar

1 tsp white vinegar

A popular dish, it is not spicy but a spoonful of fish sauce will add zest.

❋ Heat the oil in a wok or pan over medium-high heat. Coat the chicken lightly with flour and stir-fry for about 5 minutes until light brown. Remove and drain on absorbent kitchen paper.

❋ Remove all the oil except about 90 ml (6 tbsp) from the wok or pan. Add the onion and pepper and stir-fry for 1 minute. Mix in the ketchup, and add the remaining ingredients. Stir-fry for 1 minute.

❋ Return the chicken to the pan and stir-fry for about 2 minutes until the onion is tender.

CHICKEN FRIED WITH CASHEW NUTS

SERVES 4 TO 6

300 g (11 oz) boneless skinned chicken breasts, cut into slices

flour for coating

225 ml (7 fl oz) vegetable oil

4 dried red chillies, fried and cut into 1-cm (½-in) pieces

1 tbsp chopped garlic

10 spring onions, white parts, cut into 5-cm (2-in) pieces

90 ml (6 tbsp) unsalted roasted cashew nuts

1 medium onion, sliced

2 tbsp oyster sauce

1¼ tbsp soy sauce

1 tbsp sugar

freshly cooked rice to serve

Coat the chicken lightly with flour. Heat the oil in a wok or pan over medium-high heat. Add the chicken and stir-fry for about 5 minutes until light brown.

❁ Remove almost all the oil from the pan.

❁ Add the chilli and garlic to the chicken in the pan and stir-fry for 1 minute. Add all the remaining ingredients and stir-fry for about 3 minutes longer until all the ingredients are tender. Serve accompanied by rice.

CHICKEN FRIED WITH GINGER

SERVES 4	
90 ml (6 tbsp) vegetable oil	25 g (1 oz) fresh root ginger, peeled and cut into small matchsticks
1 tbsp chopped garlic	
300 g (11 oz) boneless skinned chicken breasts, cut lengthwise into 5-mm (¼-in) slices	3 fresh red chillies, each sliced into 6 strips lengthwise
25 g (1 oz) sliced button mushrooms	1 tbsp soy sauce
	2 tsp brandy
4 spring onions, cut into 2-cm (1-in) pieces	½ tsp sugar
	¼ tsp salt
1 small onion, sliced	freshly cooked rice to serve

Heat the oil in a wok or large skillet until smoking. Add the garlic and stir-fry, mixing well.

❀ Add the chicken, and stir-fry for 1 minute, then add the mushrooms. Stir for 1 minute and add the remaining ingredients.

❀ Stir-fry for 8 to 10 minutes until the chicken is cooked through and the juices run clear. Serve accompanied by rice and phrik nam plaa.

VIETNAMESE GRILLED CHICKEN

SERVES 4	
6 dried chillies, roasted, rehydrated, and seeded	1 tbsp dark brown sugar
	1 tsp turmeric
2 lemon grass stalks chopped, outer leaves removed	2 tbsp sunflower oil
	4 chicken portions, cut in half
2 garlic cloves, crushed	
5-cm (2-in) piece fresh root ginger, peeled and grated	flat-leaf parsley, lemon wedges, and sliced green chillies to garnish
1 medium onion, chopped	

If preferred, bird's-eye chillies can be substituted for the dried chillies. Depending on your heat tolerance, you should use one to three bird's-eye chillies instead of the dried chillies.

❀ Put the chillies into a food processor with the lemon grass, garlic, ginger, onions, sugar and turmeric. Blend to form a thick, chunky paste.

❀ Heat the oil in a wok or large pan. Add the paste, and stir-fry, stirring constantly, for 2 minutes. Remove from the heat, leave to cool.

❀ Then brush over the chicken portions. Cover the chicken and leave in the refrigerator for at least 3 hours.

❀ Preheat the grill to medium-high.

❀ Place the chicken on the grill rack lined with foil and grill, turning occasionally, for 15 minutes, or until the chicken is tender and the juices run clear. Serve garnished with flat-leafed parsley, lemon wedges and slices of green chillies.

Vietnamese Grilled Chicken

DUCK WITH GINGER SAUCE

SERVES 4	
vegetable oil for frying	2 tsp cornflour mixed with a little water to make a thin paste
12 thin slices fresh root ginger, peeled and shredded	
1½ tbsp chilli paste	
1½ tbsp hoisin sauce	**HO CHI WINH DUCK**
1½ tsp rice wine	salt
1½ tbsp nuoc mam sauce (page 72)	pinch of Chinese five-spice powder
1 tsp finely chopped garlic	½ tsp finely chopped fresh root ginger
1 tbsp chilli oil	½ tsp finely chopped garlic
1 tsp sugar	½ tsp hot chilli paste
salt	1 oven-ready duck, 1.75 to 2 kg (4 to 4½ lb)
225 ml (7 fl oz) chicken stock	
1 spring onion, shredded	125 ml (4 fl oz) hot water
1 fresh red chilli pepper, shredded	3 tbsp wine vinegar
	1 tbsp sugar
	red food colouring

First prepare the duck by mixing the salt, five-spice powder, ginger, garlic and chilli paste. Put the mixture inside the duck's cavity and sew up both ends. Mix the remaining ingredients together and brush over the entire surface with a pastry brush. Leave to dry on a rack with the breast uppermost for 7 hours in a cool, dry place.

❋ Preheat the oven to 200°C/400°F/Gas Mark 6. Put the rack together with the duck on a roasting pan and roast for 1 hour; reduce the heat if the skin begins to burn. (Ideally, the duck should be roasted upright in the Oriental style but most household ovens cannot accommodate an upright duck. Laying it on its back is the next best thing.)

❋ Take the cooked duck meat off the bone in as large pieces as possible and cut these into neat pieces about 1 x 2 cm (½ x 1 in).

❋ Heat the oil in a wok or large pan until smoking. Add the duck pieces and stir-fry for a few minutes; set these aside making sure to drain well.

❋ Empty and wipe the wok or pan. Heat some more oil in it, then stir-fry the ginger very briskly. Add the chilli paste and hoisin paste, return the duck to the pan.

❋ Stir in the rice wine, nuoc mam sauce, garlic, chilli oil, sugar and salt. Stir-fry for a few minutes longer.

❋ Add the chicken stock to the wok. As soon as it comes to the boil, lower the heat and simmer, uncovered, for 5 minutes.

❋ Increase the heat, add the spring onions and chilli and stir-fry quickly for 1 minute, then stir in the cornflour. Simmer for about 1 minute, stirring, then serve.

CRISPY ROAST DUCK

SERVES 4

12 wheaten crêpes

450 g (1 lb) of Ho Chi Minh Duck (see Duck with Ginger Sauce, page 104)

VEGETABLE PLATTER

1 bunch spring onions, cut into 5-cm (2-in) pieces

50 g (2 oz) fresh coriander

50 g (2 oz) fresh mint

50 g (2 oz) fresh basil

½ cucumber, peeled in alternating strips, halved lengthwise, and sliced thinly crosswise

275 g (10 oz) fresh beansprouts

bottled sweet plum sauce to accompany (this can be obtained from large supermarkets and delicatessens)

You can buy packages of the wheaten crêpes at Oriental food stores. If you can't find any, sift 225 g (8 oz) flour into a mixing bowl. Pour in 200 ml (6.5 fl oz) boiled water, stirring quickly and then stir in ½ tablespoon cold water. When cool enough, mould with your hands and form a dough. Cover with a cloth and leave for 30 minutes. Then knead lightly on a lightly floured board. Roll out the dough into a sausage shape and cut into fourteen 2-cm (1-in) portions. With the heel of your hand, flatten into circles of about 6 cm (2½ in) across.

❈ Using a pastry brush, paint half the pieces with 1 teaspoon sesame oil. Place the remaining pieces onto the oiled surfaces, making seven pairs in total. With a lightly floured rolling pin roll out

each pair to about 15 cm (6 in) across. Turn them to make them round.

❈ Dry-fry the wheaten crêpe for 1 to 2 minutes in a heavy unoiled wok or pan until they begin to turn light brown. Turn them over and repeat; they will puff up.

❈ Remove and separate the 2 thin halves; repeat until all the dough is used up. Put on a plate and cover with a cloth to prevent from drying.

❈ Steam all the crêpes in a steamer for 7 minutes just before serving with the duck.

❈ Arrange the duck on a plate. Arrange the vegetables on a plate. Put some plum sauce into a dish. Place the crêpes on a flat plate.

❈ Guests place 1 teaspoon of plum sauce with some duck and vegetables on a crêpe.

GARLIC ROASTED DUCK

1 tbsp nuoc mam sauce (page 72) or soy sauce	4 duck breast and wing portions
150 ml (¼ pt) red-wine vinegar	150 ml (¼ pt) plain yoghurt
1 onion, chopped	salt and freshly ground black pepper
12 juniper berries, crushed	
2 tsp fennel seeds	watercress to garnish
1 clove garlic, crushed	

Mix the nuoc mam sauce, vinegar, onion, juniper berries, fennel seeds and garlic together in a large bowl. Rub well into the duck portions. Cover the bowl with some clingfilm and leave in a refrigerator for 8 hours, turning over the duck pieces occasionally.

❉ Preheat the oven to 220°C/425°/Gas Mark 7.

❉ Drain the duck portions, reserving the marinade. Place the duck portions, skin side down, in a baking dish. Put in the oven for 30 minutes, basting at least once.

❉ Turn the duck portions over, baste and cook for 30 minutes longer, basting at least once. Switch off the oven but leave the duck in it.

❉ Spoon 225 ml (7 fl oz) of the marinade into a hot pan. Cover and simmer for at least 5 minutes. Strain, whisk in the yoghurt and season with salt and black pepper to taste.

❉ Serve the duck on a dish garnished with the watercress. The sauce is served in a bowl. If guests are not proficient with chopsticks, the duck should be chopped into bite-sized pieces.

RED DUCK CURRY

SERVES 6
2 l (3½ pt) thin coconut milk
1 roasted duck, boned with skin left on, cut into 1-cm (½-in) slices
15 cherry tomatoes
5 fresh large red chillies, sliced lengthwise
50 g (2 oz) sweet basil leaves
3 kaffir lime leaves, chopped
3 tbsp sugar
2 tbsp fish sauce
1 tsp salt

RED CURRY PASTE
3 stalks lemon grass, thinly sliced
60 ml (4 tbsp) chopped galangal
7 dried red chillies, roughly chopped
3 tbsp chopped garlic
1 tbsp shrimp paste
1 tsp chopped kaffir lime leaf
1 tsp chopped coriander root
1 tsp white peppercorns

This is a very popular dish in Thailand; rich and quite delicious. Serve accompanied by rice, salted eggs and sun-dried beef.

❀ Pound all the curry paste ingredients together with a mortar and pestle or in a blender to a fine paste.

❀ Heat 450 ml (¾ pt) of the coconut milk in a wok or saucepan. Add the chilli paste mixture and simmer for 5 minutes.

❀ Add the rest of the coconut milk and bring to a boil, then add the duck, cherry tomatoes and red chilli. Return to a boil and add the rest of the ingredients.

❀ Boil for 5 minutes and remove from the heat.

Meat Dishes

SPICY BEEF STEW

SERVES 4

3 tbsp vegetable oil

2 onions, finely chopped

5 cloves garlic, finely chopped

10 spring onions, dead skin peeled off

1 stalk lemon grass, cut into 5-cm (2-in) sections and crushed

1 kg (2 lb) stewing beef, cut into 2-cm (1-in) cubes

1.25 l (2 pt) water

90 ml (6 tbsp) yellow bean sauce, chopped and crushed

1 tsp chilli powder

4 star anise

2-cm (1-in) cinnamon stick

½ tsp whole peppercorns

sugar

This particular stew is, arguably, Vietnam's *boeuf à la bourguignonne*.

❉ Heat 1 tablespoon of the oil in a wok or large pan, over medium-high heat. Add the onions, garlic and whole spring onions and stir-fry for 2 minutes.

❉ Add the lemon grass and continue to stir-fry until the onions become lightly brown. Remove the spring onions and set aside.

❉ Heat the remaining oil over high heat. Stir-fry as many pieces of beef as are convenient until they are brown, turning them over from time to time. Continue until all the beef has been cooked.

❉ Add the water. Add the lemon grass mixture, yellow bean sauce, chilli powder, star anise, cinnamon, peppercorns and sugar. Bring to a boil, then cover, lower the heat and simmer for 1½ hours.

❉ Add the reserved spring onions. Cover again and let the stew continue simmering for 15 minutes longer, or until the sauce has thickened a little and the meat is tender.

SPICY BEEF STEW II

1 kg (2 lb) stewing beef, cut into 5-cm (2-in) cubes

2 lemon grass stalks, sliced paper-thin and finely chopped

2 fresh red chillies, minced

2 tsp sugar

2 tbsp grated fresh root ginger

2 tsp ground cinnamon

2 tsp curry powder

3 tbsp nuoc mam sauce (page 72) or 3 tbsp light soy sauce and ½ tsp anchovy extract

salt and freshly ground black pepper

4½ tbsp vegetable oil

1 large onion, minced

6 cloves garlic, minced

125 ml (4 fl oz) tomato purée

4 star anise

2 carrots, cut into 2-cm (1-in) chunks

2 potatoes, peeled and cut into 2-cm (1-in) chunks

1 small daikon, peeled and cut into 2-cm (1-in) chunks

Mix the beef, lemon grass, chillies, sugar, ginger, cinnamon, curry powder, nuoc mam sauce, salt and black pepper, and leave to stand for 1 hour.

❊ Heat 4 tablespoons oil in the wok over high heat. Add the beef and marinade and stir quickly to sear; this should not take much more than 2 minutes. Remove the meat to a bowl and set aside.

❊ Add a little more oil and, when hot, add the onion and garlic and stir-fry until fragrant. Add the tomato purée and stir for 2 minutes. Add the beef, star anise, a little salt and the water. Bring the mixture to a boil, then reduce the heat to low, cover the wok and simmer about 1½ hours until the beef is tender.

❊ Add the carrots and simmer for 10 minutes. Add the potatoes and simmer for 10 minutes longer. Finally, add the daikon and cook for another 10 minutes.

BEEF IN COCONUT MILK

2 tbsp vegetable oil

1 clove garlic, crushed

225 g (8 oz) topside of beef, thinly sliced

1 small onion, thinly sliced

pinch of turmeric

½ green chilli

1-cm (½-in) piece lemon grass, cut from the bottom, and thinly sliced

1 tbsp tinned coconut milk

1 tbsp peanuts, crushed

handful of fresh coriander, chopped

Heat the oil in a wok or large pan until very hot. Add the garlic.

❊ When the smell is released, add all the remaining ingredients, except the coconut milk. Stir-fry for about 3 minutes, or until the meat is cooked.

❊ Add the coconut milk and stir once. Serve garnished with crushed peanuts and chopped coriander.

STIR-FRIED BEEF WITH PEPPERS AND BAMBOO SHOOTS

SERVES 4

1 tbsp vegetable oil

450 g (1 lb) sirloin steak, thinly sliced

3 spring onions, cut in 1-cm (½-in) pieces

2 cloves garlic, crushed

100–125 g (4 oz) tinned bamboo shoots, drained and sliced

1 large green pepper, seeded and sliced

2 tbsp nuoc mam sauce (page 72)

150 ml (¼ pt) beef stock

2 tbsp sugar

2 tsp cornflour mixed with a little water

Preheat the oven on a low temperature.

❀ Heat the oil in a wok or large pan over high heat until smoking. Add the beef and stir-fry for 2 to 3 minutes, to seal in the flavours of the meat. Scoop out the beef and place it in a warm oven.

❀ Add the spring onions and garlic and stir-fry over medium heat for 3 minutes. Increase the heat to high, stir in the bamboo shoots and pepper and stir-fry for 1 to 2 minutes.

❀ Stir in the nuoc mam sauce, stock and sugar. Cover and cook for 3 minutes.

❀ Return the beef to the wok and stir for 1 minute. Add the cornflour to the beef mixture and stir constantly until the mixture thickens. Serve immediately.

CRISPY BEEF SLICES SERVED WITH A SPICY DIP

SERVES 4

450 g (1 lb) fillet steak, cut across the grain into thin slices 5 cm (2 in) long

2 eggs, beaten

1 tbsp sesame oil

1 tbsp nuoc mam sauce (page 72)

¼ tsp sugar

2 tsp finely grated fresh root ginger

1 tsp rice wine or dry sherry

vegetable oil for deep-frying

salt and freshly ground black pepper

cornflour

CHILI DIP

4 tbsp nuoc mam sauce (page 72), or soy sauce

2 tsp chilli oil

First make the dip. Put the sauce and chilli oil in a bowl and stir; set aside.

❀ Mix all the other ingredients, except the cornflour, in a second bowl and leave to marinate for 1 hour before cooking.

❀ Dredge the beef slices in cornflour. Heat the oil in a wok or large pan until smoking. Add the beef strips, a few at a time, and fry until golden brown; the colour comes from the cornflour, not the beef.

❀ Drain well on absorbent kitchen paper. Put on a dish and serve with the chilli dip.

THAI GREEN BEEF CURRY

SERVES 4

1.25 l (2 pt) thin coconut milk

300 g (11 oz) beef sirloin, cut into thin slices

2 tbsp fish sauce

½ tbsp sugar

1 large aubergine, diced

3 fresh red bird's-eye chillies, quartered lengthwise

3 kaffir lime leaves, torn into small pieces

60 ml (4 tbsp) sweet basil leaves

CHILI PASTE

20 fresh green bird's-eye chillies, chopped roughly

1 tbsp sliced shallot

1 tbsp chopped garlic

1 tbsp sliced galangal

½ stalk of lemon grass, sliced

½ tbsp coriander seeds

2 tsp salt

1 tsp shrimp paste

½ tsp chopped lime zest

½ tsp chopped coriander root or stem

6 white peppercorns, crushed

Definitely green, but rarely sweet, this is one of the basic Thai curry styles. It can be made with pork, chicken or duck as a variation from the beef used in this recipe. Serve this in bowls accompanied by rice, pickled vegetables, salted eggs and sun-dried beef.

❀ First make the chilli paste. Pound all the ingredients together, except the green chillies, to form a fine paste. Use a mortar and pestle or blender. Stir in green chillies.

❀ Heat 225 ml (7 fl oz) of the coconut milk in a wok or large pan. Add the chilli paste and simmer for 2 minutes.

❀ Add the beef and the rest of the coconut milk, then bring to the boil. Add the fish sauce and sugar, and continue boiling for 2 minutes longer. Add the aubergine and chilli and cook for 1 minute.

❀ Stir in the lime leaf and boil for 1 minute longer. Add the basil and remove from the heat. Serve at once.

COCONUT BEEF CURRY

SERVES 8

125 ml (4 fl oz) vegetable oil

300 g (11 oz) beef sirloin, cut
into very thin pieces

750 ml (1¼ pt) thin coconut
milk

1 tbsp fish sauce

2 tsp sugar

2 fresh red bird's-eye chillies,
sliced

2 kaffir lime leaves, finely
sliced

90 ml (6 tbsp) sweet basil leaves

freshly cooked rice to serve

CURRY PASTE

6 dried red chillies, roughly
chopped

7 white peppercorns

3 tbsp roughly chopped garlic

2 tbsp roughly chopped shallots

2 coriander roots, chopped
roughly

2 tsp salt

1 tsp roughly chopped galangal

1 tsp roughly chopped lemon
grass

1 tsp roughly chopped lime zest

1 tsp shrimp paste

This is one of the driest of Thai curries, and usually quite fiery.

❀ Pound all the curry paste ingredients together to form a paste with a mortar and pestle or in a blender.

❀ Heat the oil in a wok or large pan. Add the curry paste and fry for 3 to 4 minutes. Add the beef and stir-fry for 2 minutes.

❀ Add the coconut milk and boil about 15 minutes until the beef is tender.

❀ Add the fish sauce, sugar and chilli.

❀ Transfer to a serving plate and sprinkle with the lime zest and basil. Serve with rice.

RED PORK WITH RICE

SERVES 6

300 g (11 oz) pork tenderloin

1.25 l (2 pt) water

60 ml (4 tbsp) tomato purée

3 tbsp soy sauce

3 tbsp sugar

3 drops of red food colouring (optional)

1½ tbsp cornflour

75 g (3 oz) cooked rice, heated

NAM CHIM SAUCE
4 tbsp white vinegar

2 tbsp soy sauce

1 fresh red chilli, sliced thinly

¼ tsp sugar

The red-coloured marinade soaks a little way into the meat from the surface; when sliced, the red edges of the pork make this a decorative as well as tasty dish. Serve accompanied by sliced cucumber, spring onions, hard-boiled eggs, and pieces of deep-fried fresh pork fat back or pork belly.

❈ Mix together the pork, water, tomato purée, soy sauce, sugar and food colouring in a bowl. Cover and leave to marinate for 1 hour in the refrigerator.

❈ Preheat the oven to 180°C/350°F/Gas Mark 4.

❈ Put the pork mixture with its marinade in a pan and bring to a boil. Lower the heat and simmer for 30 minutes.

❈ Remove the pork and place in an ovenproof dish. Roast in the preheated oven for 10 minutes until lightly browned and glazed; reserve the cooking liquid.

❈ Mix a little of the cooking liquid with the cornflour and then stir in 450 ml (¾ pt) more liquid. Bring to a boil in a small pan to thicken, then remove from the heat.

❈ Mix together the ingredients for the nam chim sauce. Slice the pork and place on serving plates (on top of the hot rice).

❈ Spoon the cornflour sauce over the top, and serve with the nam chim sauce on the side.

PORK AND CHILLI BALLS

450 g (1 lb) lean minced pork

3 lemon grass stalks, outer
leaves removed and minced

1 tbsp red chilli paste

grated zest of 1 lime

3 tomatoes, peeled, seeded and
finely chopped

1 tsp turmeric

2 tsp minced galangal, or peeled
and crushed fresh root ginger

1 garlic clove, crushed

¼ tsp salt

oil for deep-frying

lime wedges and chilli flowers
(page 19) to garnish

Put the pork, lemon grass, red chilli paste and lime zest into a bowl. Stir in the tomatoes, turmeric, galangal or ginger, garlic and salt. Mix together well.

❀ Using slightly wet hands, form the pork mixture into small balls about the size of an apricot. Chill, covered, for at least 30 minutes.

❀ Heat the oil in a wok or deep-fat fryer to 180°C/350°F. Add the pork balls in batches and fry for 5 to 6 minutes, or until golden. Drain on absorbent kitchen paper. Serve garnished with lime wedges and chilli flowers.

BEEF RENDANG

4 dried chillies, roasted,
rehydrated, and chopped

2 shallots, chopped

1 garlic clove, crushed

2 tbsp sunflower oil

550 g (1½ lb) braising steak,
trimmed and cubed

1 tsp turmeric

600 ml (1 pt) coconut milk

2 kaffir lime leaves

juice of 2 limes

salt and pepper

50 g (2 oz) creamed coconut,
broken into small pieces

freshly cooked rice to serve

The dried chillies can be replaced with 1 or 2 bird's-eye chillies. If a thickened sauce is preferred, add 1 to 1½ tablespoons of flour when adding the turmeric. Check during cooking that the sauce is not becoming too thick; if it is, add a little more coconut milk or stock.

Look in Oriental food stores for bars of creamed coconut.

❀ Make a paste with the chillies, shallots and garlic; set aside.

❀ Heat the oil in a wok or large pan. Add the beef and fry in batches for 5 minutes, or until sealed. Remove from the pan with a slotted spoon and reserve.

❀ Add the paste to the oil remaining in the pan and gently fry for 5 minutes, stirring occasionally. Add the beef and turmeric to the pan and stir-fry for 2 minutes.

❀ Pour in the coconut milk and add the lime leaves, juice and seasonings. Bring to a boil, then cover the pan and lower the heat. Simmer for 1½ hours, or until the meat is tender.

❀ Add the creamed coconut gradually to the pan, stirring after each addition.

❀ Heat through for 5 minutes and serve with freshly cooked rice.

STIR-FRIED LAMB WITH MINT AND CHILLI

SERVES 4

1½ tbsp vegetable oil

225 g (8 oz) lean lamb, cut in fine strips

1 clove garlic, finely chopped

1 tbsp oyster sauce

1 tbsp nuoc mam sauce (page 72)

pinch of sugar

1 tbsp finely sliced bird's-eye chilli

5 tbsp fresh mint leaves, sliced if large

Heat the oil in a wok or pan over high heat. Add the lamb and stir-fry for several minutes until almost cooked.

❋ Add the garlic, oyster sauce, nuoc mam sauce, sugar and chilli and stir-fry for 2 minutes longer or so. Taste to see if extra seasoning is necessary and adjust.

❋ When the meat is cooked and tender, stir in the mint leaves. Remove from the wok or pan and serve on a dish.

LAMB IN A HOT GARLIC SAUCE

SERVES 4

225 g (8 oz) spinach or any green vegetable

2 tbsp vegetable oil

225 g (8 oz) lean lamb, thinly sliced

4 cloves garlic, finely chopped

freshly ground white pepper

½ tsp sugar

1 tbsp nuoc mam sauce (page 72), or 1 tbsp soy sauce and 1 tsp anchovy extract

1 tbsp oyster sauce

fresh sprigs of mint and/or coriander to garnish

Blanch the spinach or other vegetable in boiling water for 1 minute. Drain well and place on a serving dish.

❋ Heat the oil in a wok or large pan. Add the lamb and stir-fry until nearly cooked; this should not take more than 2 minutes.

❋ Add the garlic, pepper, sugar, nuoc mam sauce and oyster sauce, then stir-fry until the lamb is completely cooked and tender.

❋ Pour the lamb and sauce over the greens. Garnish with mint and/or coriander sprigs.

Lamb in hot garlic sauce

SPICY GRILLED MEAT ON A BED OF VERMICELLI

225 g (8 oz) rice vermicelli

450 g (1 lb) fresh fat bacon with rind, cut against the grain into 5-mm (¼-in) strips, about 5 cm (2in) long

450 g (1 lb) beef, minced

8 cloves garlic, crushed

CARAMEL SAUCE

110 g (4 oz) sugar

60 ml (4 tbsp) nuoc mam sauce (page 72)

4 spring onions, thinly sliced

freshly ground black pepper

Soak the vermicelli in warm water until soft. Drain and set aside.

❋ Make the caramel sauce by swirling the sugar gently in a wok over hot heat; be careful not to let the sugar blacken but ignore the smoke. Remove the wok from the heat and add the nuoc mam.

❋ Return the wok to low heat and boil gently until the sugar dissolves. Add the spring onions and pepper and stir. Set aside.

❋ Put 24 bamboo skewers into water and allow to soak for at least 30 minutes.

❋ Meanwhile, put the pork and beef into 2 separate bowls. Put the garlic and half of the caramel sauce onto the beef. Put the remainder of the caramel sauce onto the pork. Blend both with your hands and leave to stand for 30 minutes. Make 24 meatballs out of the beef.

❋ Skewer the beef balls and pork slices. Cook under a hot grill for 15 to 20 minutes, turning frequently. Serve on the bed of vermicelli.

STIR-FRIED PORK SLICES AND CELERY

SERVES 4

2 tbsp vegetable oil

450 g (1 lb) lean pork, sliced thinly

1 tsp soy sauce

1 tsp sugar

225 g (8 oz) button mushrooms

335 g (12 oz) cabbage, finely chopped

4 celery sticks, thinly sliced

1 tbsp nuoc mam sauce (page 72)

3 tbsp chicken stock

cornflour

salt

freshly cooked rice or noodles to serve

Preheat the oven to its lowest setting.

❋ Heat 1 tablespoon of the oil in a wok or large pan until smoking. Add the pork and stir-fry over highest heat for 2½ minutes or longer if the pork needs more cooking.

❋ Add the soy sauce and sugar and stir with the pork for 2 minutes longer. Scoop into a bowl and keep in a warm oven.

❋ Wipe the wok or pan and heat the remaining oil until smoking. Add the mushrooms, cabbage and celery and stir-fry for 1½ minutes.

❋ Add the nuoc mam sauce, if using, and stock and stir-fry for another minute. Cover and leave to cook for 2 minutes longer.

❋ Add the pork with the cornflour and salt to taste. Stir and mix thoroughly for a minute or so. Serve immediately with rice or noodles.

VIETNAMESE PORK AU CARAMEL

SERVES 4

60 ml (4 tbsp) sugar

2 tbsp water

450 g (1 lb) boneless leg of pork, cut into large cubes

3 daikon (white Chinese radishes), peeled and thinly sliced

½ onion, chopped

6 tbsp nuoc mam sauce (page 72) or soy sauce

freshly ground black pepper

Put the sugar in a wok or large pan over low heat. Heat gently until it starts to smell as though it is burning. Stir in the water very carefully so the mixture does not break up.
❁ Add the pork and daikon and cover with water. Add the remaining ingredients and bring to a boil. Lower the heat, cover and simmer for about 1 hour, or until the pork is tender.

Minced Pork, Prawns and Pineapple Salad with Fish Sauce Dressing

SERVES 4

450 g (1 lb) boneless lean pork,
minced or finely chopped

2 tbsp water

225 g (8 oz) cooked prawns

2 tbsp lemon juice

2 tbsp nuoc mam sauce
(page 72)

½ tsp chilli powder

1 tsp finely sliced fresh red chilli

2 tbsp finely sliced onion

2 tbsp spring onions cut into
1-cm (½-in) pieces

2 tbsp roasted peanuts

2 slices pineapple, roughly
chopped

2 tbsp finely sliced fresh root
ginger

1 tbsp chopped fresh mint leaves

2 tbsp fresh coriander leaves
and stem, chopped

6 large lettuce leaves

GARNISH

roasted peanuts

1 tbsp finely sliced fresh root
ginger

pinch of chilli powder

1 red bird's-eye chilli, sliced

sprigs of mint

sprigs of coriander

spring onion (page 19)

chilli flowers (page 19)

Heat a wok over medium heat. Add the pork and water and cook, stirring frequently, until the pork is cooked through and no longer pink. Remove from the heat.

❀ Add the prawns, lemon juice, nuoc mam sauce and dried and fresh chillies and stir. Add the onion, spring onions, peanuts, pineapple, ginger, mint and coriander leaves. Toss lightly.

❀ Serve on a bed of lettuce leaves. Decorate with the garnish: peanuts, ginger, chilli, sprigs of mint and coriander, spring onion brush, and chilli flowers. Serve immediately.

MINCED PORK AND PRAWNS ON SUGAR CANE

SERVES 4

1 tbsp dried shrimp (optional)

225 g (8 oz) shelled prawns

175 g (6 oz) pork, minced

1 small onion, finely chopped

2 tbsp finely chopped coriander leaves

salt and freshly ground black pepper

1 tbsp nuoc mam sauce (page 72)

1 egg, beaten

4 x 15-cm (6-in) pieces of sugar cane or bamboo skewers

flour or cornflour (optional)

vegetable oil for deep-frying (optional)

Boston lettuce

If using dried shrimp, soak them for about 1 hour in warm water. Squeeze out the excess water and chop finely. Rinse the fresh prawns and chop finely.

❀ Put the minced pork into a large bowl. Add the onion, fresh prawns and dried shrimp, salt and pepper and nuoc mam sauce.

❀ Pour the egg into the pork and shrimp mixture and mix well with your hand; the mixture should come together so that it can be moulded around the piece of sugar cane or around bamboo skewers. If it is too runny, sift in some cornflour.

❀ Peel the sugar cane, leaving 2 cm (1 in) of the green covering on at each end, or 5 cm (2 in) at one end. Mould the mixture on to the peeled part of the sugar cane.

❀ Preheat the grill to medium-high.

❀ Grill the sticks under the grill, turning to ensure evenness in the cooking. Make sure that the sugar cane does not burn. Alternatively, deep-fry in hot oil for 4 to 5 minutes.

❀ Serve on a bed of lettuce. The sugar cane should be chewed or sucked as you eat the shrimp and pork.

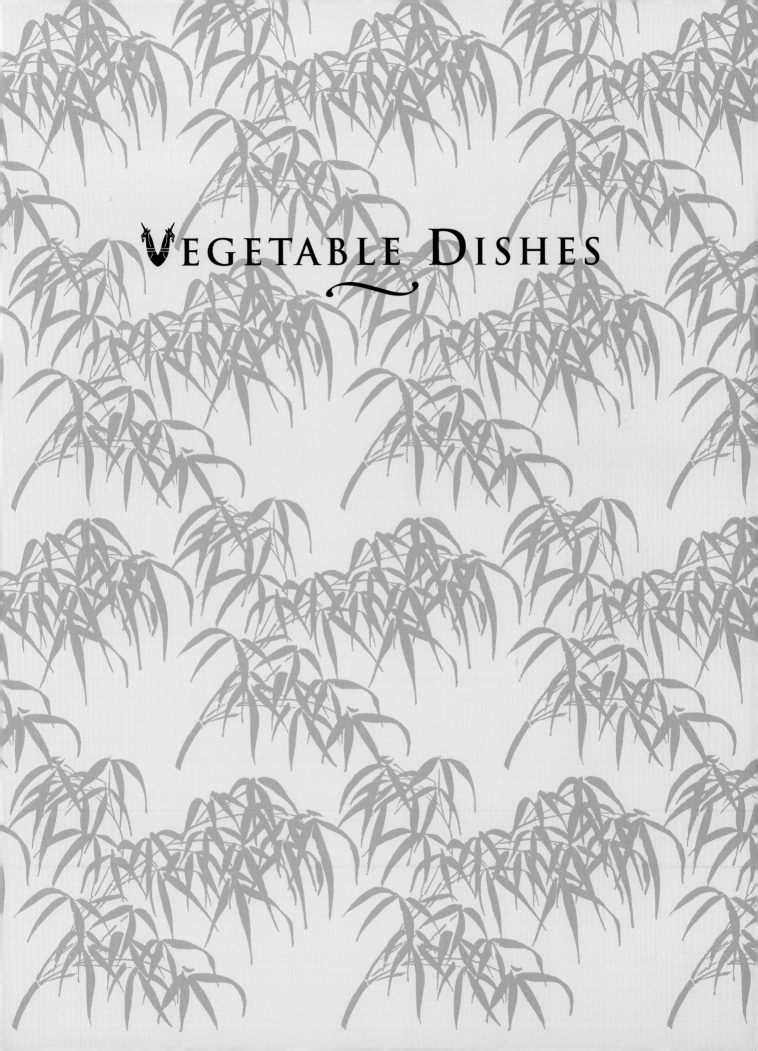

VEGETABLE DISHES

STIR-FRIED MIXED VEGETABLES

SERVES 4	
65 g (2½ oz) mange tout	65 g (2½ oz) fresh baby corn, halved
110 g (4 oz) sliced kale or cabbage	125 ml (4 fl oz) chicken stock
110 g (4 oz) sliced cabbage	½ tsp ground white pepper
110 g (4 oz) sliced broccoli flowerets and stems	60 ml (4 tbsp) peanut or corn oil
110 g (4 oz) cauliflower florets	3 tbsp finely chopped garlic
110 g (4 oz) asparagus cut into 5-cm (2-in) pieces	4 tbsp oyster sauce
110 g (4 oz) shredded Chinese cabbage	1¼ tsp soy sauce
50 g (2 oz) halved button mushrooms	freshly cooked rice to serve

Mix all the vegetables together in a bowl, pour over the stock and add the white pepper.

❋ Heat a wok or pan until lightly smoking. Add the oil. When it is hot, add the garlic and stir well.

❋ Add the vegetables and liquid all at once (watch for splashing), and stir-fry 3 to 4 minutes until they are almost all tender; the vegetables should still be slightly crisp.

❋ Add the oyster sauce and soy sauce, mix well and continue stir-frying for 1 minute longer. Serve at once, accompanied by rice; this dish goes well with most main courses.

Vegetarian "Lion Head" Casserole

SERVES 4

4 cakes of tofu

100–125 g (4 oz) fried gluten

4 or 5 dried Chinese mushrooms, soaked in warm water for 30 minutes and drained

50 g (2 oz) bamboo shoots

2 cooked carrots, chopped

1 tbsp salt

1 tsp finely chopped fresh root ginger

2 to 3 tbsp ground rice or breadcrumbs

1 tbsp cornflour

2 tsp sesame oil

flour for dusting

6 cabbage or lettuce hearts, cored

1 tsp sugar

5 large cabbage leaves

2 tbsp rice wine or dry sherry

vegetable oil for deep-frying

1 tsp freshly ground white pepper

"Lion's head" in Chinese cuisine means pork meatballs with cabbage. Here the "meatballs" are made entirely from vegetables.

❀ Squeeze the tofu, using a piece of muslin, to wring out the excess liquid, then mash.

❀ Finely chop the gluten, mushrooms and bamboo shoots. Place them with the mashed bean curd in a large mixing bowl.

❀ Add the carrots, 1 teaspoon of the salt, the root ginger, ground rice, cornflour, and sesame oil and blend everything together until smooth.

❀ Shape 10 "meatballs" from this mixture and place them on a plate lightly dusted with flour.

❀ Heat the oil in a wok or deep-fat fryer. When hot, deep-fry the "meatballs" for about 3 minutes, stirring very gently to make sure that they are not stuck together. Scoop out with a slotted spoon or

strainer and drain well on absorbent kitchen paper.

❀ Pour off the excess oil, leaving about 2 tablespoons in the wok. Stir-fry the cabbage hearts with a little salt and sugar. Add about 600 ml (1 pt) water and bring to a boil. Lower the heat and let the mixture simmer.

❀ Meanwhile, line the bottom of a flameproof casserole with the cabbage leaves and place the "meatballs" on top. Pour the cabbage hearts with the soup into the casserole and add the remaining salt, ground pepper and rice wine. Cover, bring to a boil, lower the heat and simmer for 10 minutes.

❀ To serve, take off the lid and rearrange the cabbage hearts so that they appear between the "meatballs" in a star-shaped pattern.

CHINESE CABBAGE
CASSEROLE

*450 g (1 lb) Chinese cabbage,
rinsed and finely chopped*

*2 cakes fresh tofu, cut into 24
pieces*

*3 tbsp vegetable oil, plus extra
for frying the tofu*

1 tsp salt

1 tsp sugar

*1 large carrot, peeled and cut
into diamond shapes*

2 tbsp soy sauce

2 tbsp rice wine or dry sherry

1 tsp sesame oil

Heat a small amount of vegetable oil in a pan. Add the tofu cubes and gently fry them until they are golden brown on all sides. Drain well on absorbent kitchen paper.

❁ Heat 3 tablespoons oil in a hot wok or large pan. Add the cabbage, salt and sugar and stir-fry for a minute or so.

❁ Transfer it to a flameproof casserole and cover the cabbage with the tofu, carrots, soy sauce and sherry.

❁ Place the casserole over high heat, cover and bring to a boil. Lower the heat and simmer for 15 minutes.

❁ Stir in the sesame oil. Add a little water, if necessary, and simmer for a few more minutes. Serve hot.

CHINESE CABBAGE AND MUSHROOMS

SERVES 4

6 to 8 dried Chinese mushrooms, soaked in warm water for 30 minutes

450 g (1 lb) Chinese cabbage leaves

3 tbsp vegetable oil

1 tsp salt

1 tsp sugar

1 tbsp soy sauce

1 tsp sesame oil

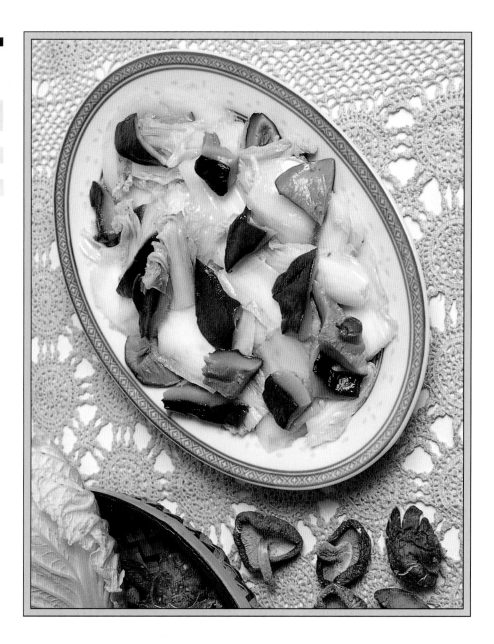

Squeeze the mushrooms dry and discard the hard stems; reserve the soaking water. Cut each mushroom into quarters.

❉ Cut the cabbage leaves into pieces about the size of large postage stamps.

❉ Heat the oil in a wok or large pan.

❉ Add the cabbage and the mushrooms and stir-fry until soft. Add the salt, sugar and soy sauce and continue stir-frying for 1½ minutes longer.

❉ Mix in some of the water in which the mushrooms were soaked and the sesame seed oil. Serve at once.

SHREDDED CABBAGE WITH RED AND GREEN PEPPERS

SERVES 4

3 tbsp vegetable oil

450 g (1 lb) white cabbage, cored and thinly shredded

1 green pepper, seeded and thinly shredded

1 red pepper, seeded and thinly shredded

1 tsp salt

1 tsp sesame oil

Heat the oil in a wok or large pan until hot.

❁ Add the cabbage and the peppers and stir-fry for 1 to 1½ minutes.

❁ Add the salt and stir a few more times. Add the sesame oil to garnish and serve hot or at room temperature.

GREEN BEANS IN GARLIC SAUCE

SERVES 3 TO 4

400 g (14 oz) green beans, topped and tailed

3 tbsp vegetable oil

1 large or 2 small cloves garlic, crushed and finely chopped

1 tsp salt

1 tsp sugar

1 tbsp soy sauce

Leave the beans whole if they are young and tender, otherwise cut them in half.

❁ Blanch the beans in a pan of lightly salted boiling water. Drain and plunge in cold water to stop the cooking and to preserve the beans' bright green colour.

❁ Heat the oil in a hot wok or large pan. When it starts to smoke, add the garlic to flavour the oil.

❁ Before the colour of the garlic turns dark brown, add the beans and stir-fry for about 1 minute. Add the salt, sugar and soy sauce and continue stir-frying for another minute at most. Serve hot or at room temperature.

THE THREE DELICACIES

SERVES 4

100–125 g (4 oz) oyster or straw mushrooms

4 tbsp vegetable oil

250 g (9 oz) tinned bamboo shoots, well drained and thinly sliced

275 g (10 oz) fried gluten (page 11), or deep-fried tofu

1½ tsp salt

1 tsp sugar

1 tbsp soy sauce

1 tsp sesame oil

fresh coriander leaves to garnish (optional)

The Chinese like to combine a number of different ingredients in a harmonious balance of colour, texture, and flavour and then give the dish a poetic descriptive name, such as Four Treasures, Two Winters or Three Delicacies. They are also superstitious and consider certain numbers lucky, particularly two, three, four, five and eight.

This dish can also be served cold. In that case, you might like to separate the three main ingredients, arrange them in three neat rows and garnish with fresh coriander leaves.

✤ Heat the oil in a hot wok or pan, swirling it so that most of the surface is well greased. When the oil starts to smoke, add the bamboo shoots and mushrooms and stir-fry for about 1 minute.

✤ Add the gluten or tofu with the salt, sugar, and soy sauce. Continue stir-frying for 1 to 1½ minutes longer, adding a little water if necessary.

✤ Finally, add the sesame oil, and serve hot.

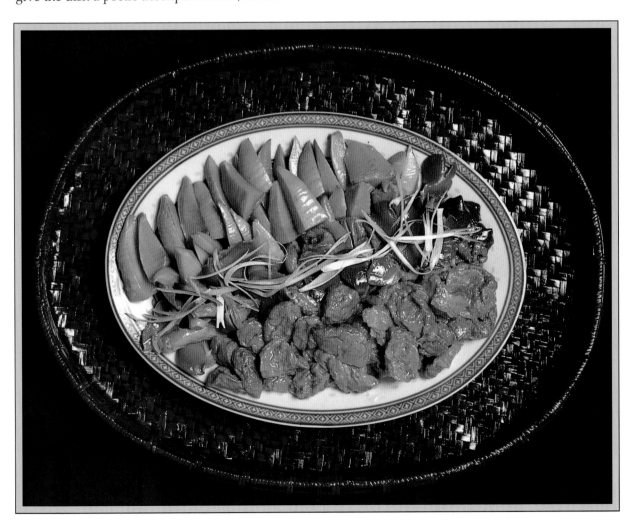

BRAISED BAMBOO SHOOTS

SERVES 4

3 tbsp vegetable oil

450 g (1 lb) tinned slender bamboo shoots, well drained and thinly sliced lengthwise

2 tbsp rice wine or dry sherry

1 tbsp sugar

3 tbsp soy sauce

2 tsp sesame oil

Heat the oil in a hot wok or pan. Add the bamboo shoots and stir-fry until well covered with oil. Add the wine, sugar and soy sauce and continue stir-frying.

❀ Braise for 3 to 4 minutes, or until almost all the liquid has evaporated. Add the sesame oil and serve hot or at room temperature.

133

STIR–FRIED BAMBOO SHOOTS WITH WINTER MUSHROOMS

SERVES 4

25 g (1 oz) dried Chinese mushrooms

2 tbsp vegetable oil

225 g (8 oz) winter bamboo shoots, drained and sliced same size as mushrooms

3 tbsp soy sauce

1 tsp sugar

4 tbsp mushroom stock

1 tsp cornflour mixed with 2 tsp water

1 tsp sesame oil

Select mushrooms of uniform, small size. Soak them in warm water for about half an hour, then squeeze them dry and keep the soaking liquid as mushroom stock. Strain the liquid through muslin and set aside.

❀ Heat the oil until it smokes. Stir-fry the mushrooms and bamboo shoots for about 1 minute.

❀ Add the soy sauce and sugar and stir a few more times.

❀ Add the mushroom stock and bring to a boil, then continue stir-frying for about 2 minutes. Add the cornflour and water mixture and blend well.

❀ Add the sesame oil and serve.

"BUDDHA'S DELIGHT" — EIGHT TREASURES OF CHINESE VEGETABLES

SERVES 4	
15 g (½ oz) dried lily buds	90 ml (6 tbsp) white nuts
15 g (½ oz) dried wood ears	1½ tsp salt
7.5 g (¼ oz) dried black moss	1 tsp sugar
4 tbsp vegetable oil	1 tbsp soy sauce
50 g (2 oz) bamboo shoots, thinly sliced	1 tsp cornflour mixed with 1 tbsp cold water to form a smooth paste
50 g (2 oz) lotus root, thinly	
50 g (2 oz) straw mushrooms	2 tsp sesame oil
15 g (½ oz) dried tofu skin sticks, cut into short pieces	

The original recipe calls for eighteen different ingredients to represent the eighteen Buddhas. Over the years, however, this was reduced to eight, usually consisting half of dried and half of fresh vegetables.

❀ Soak the dried vegetables separately in cold water overnight or in warm water for 1 hour.

❀ Heat a wok or large pan. When it is hot, put in about half of the oil and wait until it smokes. Stir-fry all the dried vegetables with a little salt for about 1 minute; remove and set aside.

❀ Add and heat the remaining oil. Stir-fry the rest of the vegetables and the tofu pieces and the salt for about 1 minute.

❀ Add the partly cooked dried vegetables, the sugar and soy sauce stirring constantly. If the contents start to dry out, pour in a little water.

❀ When the vegetables are tender, add the cornflour and water mixture to thicken the gravy. Add the sesame oil just before serving. This dish can be served hot or at room temperature.

BRAISED "THREE PRECIOUS JEWELS"

SERVES 4

4 tbsp vegetable oil

2 cakes of tofu, cubed

225 g (8 oz) broccoli, cut into flowerets and sliced, or mange tout

1 large carrot, peeled and chopped

1 tsp salt

1 tsp sugar

1 tbsp soy sauce

1 tbsp rice wine or dry sherry

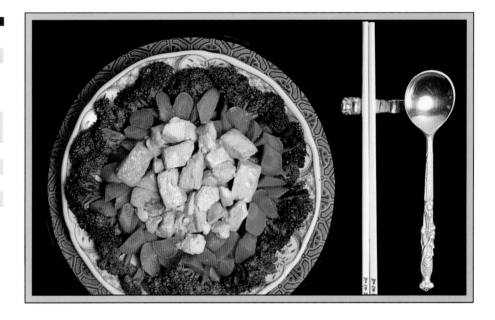

Heat about half of the oil in a hot wok or large pan. Add the tofu pieces and shallow-fry on both sides until golden. Drain well on absorbent kitchen paper and set aside.

❀ Heat the rest of the oil. When very hot, stir-fry the broccoli and carrots for 1 to 1½ minutes.

❀ Add the tofu, salt, sugar, wine and soy sauce and continue stir-frying, adding a little water if necessary, for 2 to 3 minutes if you like the broccoli and carrots to be crunchy. If not, cook for 1 to 2 minutes longer. This dish is best served hot.

STIR-FRIED GREEN AND RED PEPPERS

SERVES 4

1 large or 2 small red peppers, seeded and cut into diamond shapes

3 tbsp vegetable oil

1 tsp salt

1 tsp sugar

Heat the oil in a hot wok or pan, swirling it so most of the surface is well greased. When the oil starts to smoke, add the peppers and stir-fry until each piece is coated with oil.

❀ Add the salt and sugar. Continue stir-frying for about 1 minute and serve if you like your vegetables crunchy and crisp. If not, you can cook them for another minute or so until the skin of the peppers becomes slightly wrinkled. Add a little water if necessary during the last stage of cooking. Serve immediately.

Stir-fried Green and Red Peppers

STIR-FRIED GREENS

SERVES 4 TO 6

3 tbsp vegetable oil

300 g (11 oz) morning glory
(swamp cabbage) leaves and
stems cut into 15-cm (4-in)
pieces

125 ml (4 fl oz) chicken stock

2 tbsp marinated soybeans

1 tbsp chopped garlic

hot steamed rice to serve

Possibly the fastest dish to cook in Thailand, let alone anywhere else, this is properly made with the water plant variously know in English as morning glory, swamp cabbage or water convolvulus. As this is a Chinese dish in origin, look for this in a Chinese supermarket—or else substitute spinach.

❁ Heat the oil in a wok or pan until very hot. Add all the ingredients at once (watch for splattering), and stir-fry for about 2 minutes until the leaves are wilted and tender.

❁ Serve accompanied by steamed rice.

ROASTED AUBERGINE SALAD

1 aubergine, about 300 g
(11 oz)

30 ml (2 tbsp) minced pork

50 g (2 oz) dried shrimps,
rinsed in hot water and drained

3 tbsp vegetable oil

2 shallots, sliced

5 fresh green bird's-eye chillies,
roughly chopped

2 tbsp lime juice

1 tsp fish sauce

¼ tsp sugar

freshly cooked rice to serve

Roast the aubergine in a preheated 180°C/350°F/Gas Mark 4 oven for 15 to 20 minutes until soft. Set aside and let cool, then remove the skin and slice into 5-cm (1-in) pieces.

❁ Heat a little oil in a wok or pan. Add the pork and stir-fry for about 10 minutes until it is cooked through and no longer pink.

❁ Combine the aubergine, pork, dried shrimp and all the remaining ingredients together well in a bowl. Serve accompanied by rice.

SZECHWAN TOFU

SERVES 4

7.5 g (¼ oz) dried wood ears or dried Chinese mushrooms, soaked in warm water for about 30 minutes and drained

3 cakes of tofu, cut into 1-cm (½-in) cubes

3 tbsp vegetable oil

1 leek or 2 to 3 spring onions, cut into short pieces

1 tsp salted black beans

1 tbsp chilli bean paste

2 tbsp rice wine or dry sherry

1 tbsp soy sauce

1 tsp cornflour mixed with 1 tbsp cold water to form a smooth paste

freshly ground Szechwan pepper to garnish

Squeeze the mushrooms dry. Discard any hard stems and cut them into small pieces, retaining the soaking water for later use.

❁ Blanch the tofu cubes in a pan of boiling water for 2 to 3 minutes, then remove with a slotted spoon and drain well.

❁ Heat the oil in a hot wok or pan until it smokes. Add the leeks or spring onions and the wood ears or mushrooms and stir-fry for 1 minute.

❁ Add the salted black beans, crush them with the scooper or spatula and blend well. Add the tofu, the chilli bean paste, rice wine or sherry and soy sauce and continue stir-frying to blend.

❁ Add a little water and cook for 3 to 4 minutes longer. Finally add the cornflour-and-water mixture to thicken the sauce.

❁ Serve hot with freshly ground Szechwan pepper as garnish.

FU-YUNG TOFU

SERVES 4

1 cake tofu, cut into long, thin strips

4 egg whites

1 tbsp cornflour mixed with 2 tbsp water

60 ml (4 tbsp) milk

vegetable oil for deep-frying

1 Romaine lettuce heart, separated into leaves

1 spring onion, finely chopped

½ tsp fresh root ginger, finely chopped

1 tsp salt

100–125 g (4 oz) shelled peas, thawed if frozen

1 tsp sesame oil

In most Chinese restaurants, *fu yung* means "omelette," but strictly speaking, it should mean scrambled egg whites with a creamy texture.

❉ Blanch the tofu in a pan of salted boiling water to harden. Remove with a slotted spoon and drain well.

❉ Lightly beat the egg whites in a bowl. Stir in the cornflour mixture and milk.

❉ Coat the tofu cubes with the egg white mixture.

❉ Heat the oil in a wok or large pan until it is very hot. Turn off the heat and let the oil cool a bit before adding the tofu cubes, then fry them for 1 to 1½ minutes. Scoop out with a slotted spoon and drain well on absorbent kitchen paper.

❉ Pour off the excess oil, leaving about 1 tablespoon in the wok or pan. Increase the heat and stir-fry the lettuce heart with a pinch of salt. Remove and set aside on a serving dish.

❉ Heat another tablespoon of oil in the wok until it is smoking. Add the spring onion and root ginger, followed by the peas, salt and a little water

❉ When the mixture starts to boil, add the tofu strips. Blend well and add the sesame oil. Serve on the bed of lettuce heart.

141

STIR-FRIED MANGE TOUT WITH CHINESE MUSHROOMS

SERVES 4

6 to 8 dried Chinese mushrooms, soaked in warm water for 30 minutes and drained

225 g (8 oz) mange tout, trimmed

3 tbsp vegetable oil

1 tsp salt

1 tsp sugar

A little cornflour mixed with cold water can be added to thicken the liquid at the last minute, if you prefer a thicker sauce.

❀ Squeeze dry the mushrooms and discard the hard stems, reserving the soaking water. Cut each mushroom into small pieces.

❀ If the mange tout are large, they should be snapped in half; smaller ones can be left whole.

❀ Heat the oil in a very hot wok or large pan until smoking. Add the mange tout and stir-fry for a few seconds.

❀ Add the mushrooms, the salt and sugar and continue stir-frying for about 30 seconds. Add a little of the water in which the mushrooms were soaked. Serve as soon as the liquid starts to boil.

142

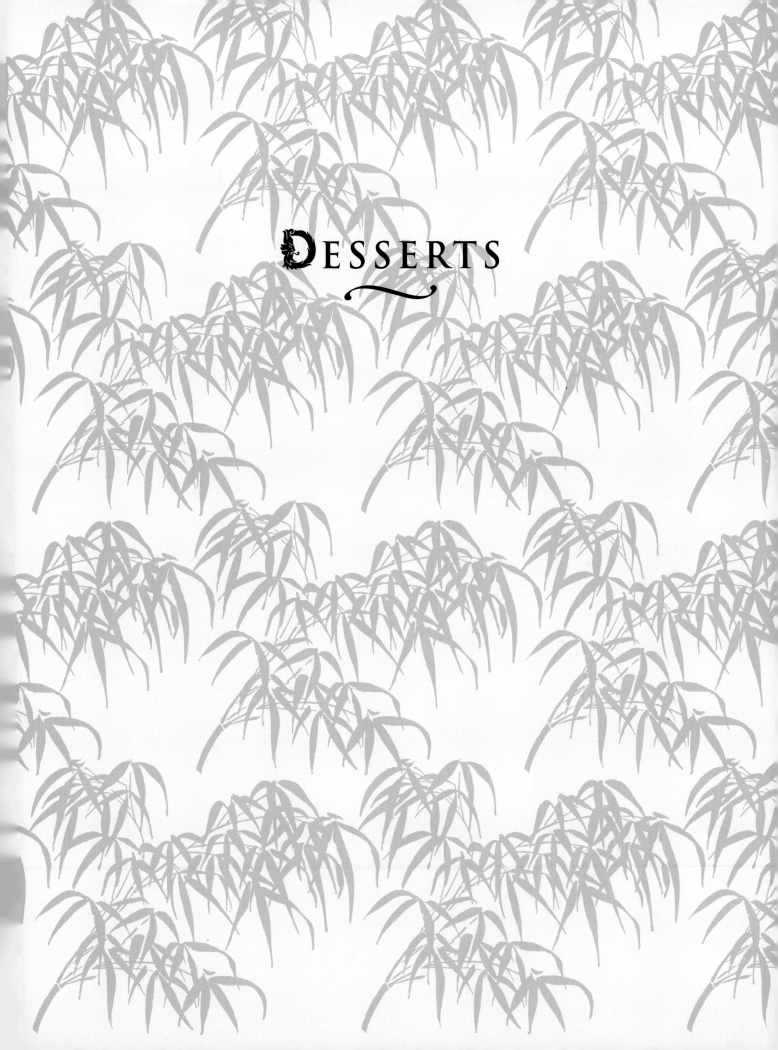

DESSERTS

LYCHEE SLAP

1 medium jar Chinese preserved ginger, drained

100–125 g (4-oz) tin lychee

1 tbsp ginger wine

Insert a piece of the drained ginger into each lychee.

❊ Mix the liquid from the ginger and the lychee syrup together. Add the ginger wine. Pour over the stuffed lychee. Cover and chill until ready to serve.

LYCHEE AND LIME SORBET

450 g (1 lb) fresh lychee

juice of 1 lime

150 g (5 oz) icing sugar, sifted

1 egg white

Peel the lychee and remove the seeds.

❀ Place the flesh in a blender with the lime juice and icing sugar. Process until smooth.

❀ Pour into a freezerproof container and freeze until slushy, then beat well. Repeat this twice.

❀ Beat the egg white until firm, then fold it into the sorbet. Return to the freezer for at least several hours until solid.

❀ Serve in small scoops with slices of fresh mango or other suitable exotic fruit, or with another fruit sorbet, such as mango or kiwi.

BANANAS IN A RICH
COCONUT SAUCE

SERVES 4

375 ml (12 fl oz) coconut milk

2 tbsp sugar

salt

*6 large bananas, peeled and
sliced diagonally about
1.5-cm (¾-in) thick*

*ice cream or whipped cream
to serve*

Heat the coconut milk in a small saucepan. Add the sugar and salt. Bring to a boil, then lower the heat and simmer for 2 minutes. ❀ Remove the pan from the heat and stir in the banana slices. Return to a boil for a few seconds to coat the bananas. Serve with ice cream or whipped cream.

FRIED BANANAS

450 g (16 oz) rice flour

225 ml (7 fl oz) water

40 g (1½ oz) unsweetened
grated coconut

3 tbsp flour

3 tbsp sugar

2 tbsp sesame seeds

2 tsp baking powder

1 tsp salt

about 1¼ l (2⅓ pt) vegetable oil
for deep-frying

450 g (1 lb) small, slightly
green bananas, quartered

If at all possible, buy small, fragrant bananas for this (and other) banana desserts.

❀ Mix together well all the ingredients, except the oil and bananas.

❀ Heat the oil in a wok or a heavy-bottomed saucepan to about 180°C/350°F.

❀ Dip the banana pieces into the coconut batter and then deep-fry for about 3 minutes until brown but not dark. Turn over and fry for 2 minutes longer.

❀ Remove with a slotted spoon and drain on absorbent kitchen paper. Serve immediately.

BAKED BANANAS WITH MANGO

SERVES 4

4 bananas

2 small mangoes

2 tbsp lemon juice

1 lime

cream and dark brown sugar
to serve

Preheat the oven to 200°C/400°F/Gas Mark 6.

❉ Place the unpeeled bananas on a baking sheet and bake for 10 minutes until the skins are black.

❉ Meanwhile, cut the mangoes in half each side of the seed and cut into wedges, removing the peel if preferred.

❉ Remove the bananas from the oven, cut a sliver of skin from the base of each banana so that they sit upright, make 2 parallel cuts along the top of each, then cut away the center section of skin. Sprinkle the banana flesh with lemon juice.

❉ Place the bananas in serving dishes and arrange the mango wedges along the top. Cut the lime into slices, halve each slice and arrange alternately between the mango wedges.

❉ Serve with cream, sprinkled with dark brown sugar.

TOFFEE BANANAS

SERVES 4

1 egg

2 tbsp flour

vegetable oil for deep-frying

4 bananas, peeled and
quartered

4 tbsp sugar

1 tbsp cold water

Beat the egg, add the flour and mix well to make a smooth batter.

❉ Heat the oil in a wok or deep-fat fryer. Coat each piece of banana with batter, dripping off any excess. Deep-fry until golden, then remove with a slotted spoon and drain.

❉ Pour off the excess oil, leaving about 1 tablespoon of oil in the wok or fryer. Add the sugar and water and stir over medium heat to dissolve the sugar.

❉ Continue stirring and when the sugar has caramelized, add the hot banana pieces. Coat well and remove.

❉ Dip the hot bananas in cold water to harden the toffee. Serve immediately.

Toffee Bananas

MANGO ICE CREAM

*4 ripe mangoes, or 100–125 g
(4 oz) tin sliced mango*

*225 g (8 oz) sugar or 100–125
g (4 oz) if using canned mango*

1 tbsp lemon juice

*1 tbsp unflavoured powdered
gelatin, dissolved in 3 tbsp
water*

*375 ml (12 fl oz) double cream,
whipped until stiff*

GARNISH

extra mango slices

sprigs of fresh mint

Peel and cut the mangoes, discarding the
seeds. Place the flesh in a bowl and add the
sugar, lemon juice and dissolved gelatin. Mix
thoroughly, making sure that the sugar is
dissolved.

❀ Fold the whipped cream into the mango
mixture. Spoon into a freezerproof container and
place in the freezer until half-frozen.

❀ Put the ice-cream mixture in a blender or food
processor and process until smooth. Return to the
freezer until solid.

❀ Serve in scoops, garnished with freshly sliced
mango and sprigs of fresh mint.

RED BEAN PASTE ROLLS

SERVES 4

225 g (8 oz) flour

125 ml (4 fl oz) boiling water

3 tbsp vegetable oil

1 egg, lightly beaten

4 to 5 tbsp sweetened red bean paste or chestnut purée

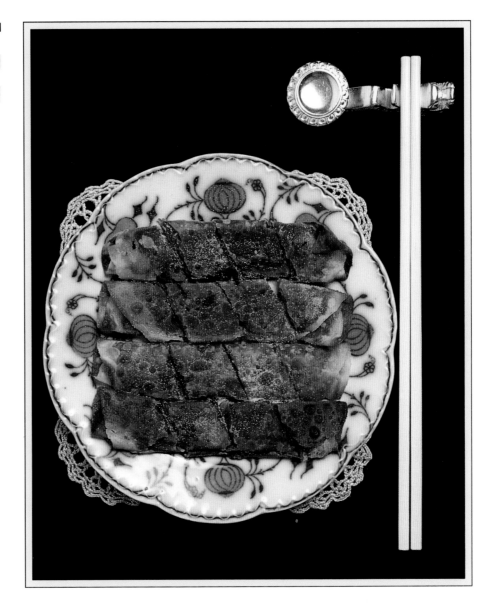

Sift the flour into a mixing bowl and very gently pour in the boiling water. Add about 1 teaspoon oil and the beaten egg.

❁ Knead into a firm dough and then divide it into 2 equal portions. Roll out each portion into a long "sausage" shape on a lightly floured surface and cut it into 4 to 6 pieces. Using the palm of your hand, press each piece into a flat pancake.

❁ On a lightly floured surface, flatten each pancake into a 15-cm (6-in) circle with a rolling pin and roll gently.

❁ Place an ungreased pan over high heat. When hot, reduce the heat to low and place one pancake at a time in the pan. Turn it over when little brown spots appear on the underside. Remove and keep under a damp cloth until you have finished making all the pancakes.

❁ Spread 2 tablespoons red bean paste or chestnut purée over 80 per cent of the pancake surface and roll it over 3 or 4 times to form a flattened roll. Repeat until all the dough is used.

❁ Heat the oil in the wiped-out pan and shallow-fry the rolls until golden brown, turning them over once.

❁ Cut each roll into 4 pieces. Serve hot or cold.

COCONUT CUSTARD

SERVES 4

225 ml (7 fl oz) thick coconut milk

4 eggs, beaten

100–125 g (4 oz) sugar

Beat the coconut milk, eggs and sugar together until the sugar dissolves and the mixture is thoroughly blended.

❋ Strain the mixture through muslin; the result should be perfectly smooth.

❋ Place a serving bowl on top of a wooden trivet in a wok and test it for firmness. Pour the mixture into the serving bowl. Pour some water into the wok and bring to a boil. Place the serving bowl on the wooden trivet and steam for 10 to 15 minutes until the mixture is firm.

❋ Alternatively, pour the mixture into 4 individual bowls and steam in a large bamboo steamer.

GOLD THREADS

SERVES 6

4 egg shells

1.3 kg (3 lb) sugar

2.5 l (4 pt) water

1 tsp vanilla extract or
jasmine water

15 egg yolks, duck if available,
lightly whisked

Use a metal cup measure or a well washed empty tin and punch about 25 small holes into its base with a nail and hammer; wash and dry well.

❊ Put the egg shells, sugar and water in a pan and bring to a boil, lower the heat and simmer until reduced by about half. Strain the liquid through muslin.

❊ Bring the strained syrup back to a simmer, and add the extract. Then, pour the beaten egg yolks through the "strainer" over the simmering sugar syrup; cook in batches of about ½ tin at a time. Let cook for 1 minute and remove with a slotted spoon or strainer.

❊ Repeat the process until all the egg is used, placing the threads on a rack to drain.

❊ When cool, gather into small bundles and serve or refrigerate until ready to use.

SWEET BLACKENED JELLY

SERVES 6 TO 8

hairy brown coating from outside of coconuts

1.75 l (3 pt) water

450 g (16 oz) rice flour

½ tbsp tapioca flour

600 g (1¼ lb) sugar

225 g (8 oz) unsweetened grated coconut

¼ tsp salt

This unusual dessert must be one of the few dishes anywhere in the world that makes use of the outside of a mature coconut—something that, fortunately, is usually readily available in the West!

❋ Take the coconut "hair" and roast it in a preheated 190°C/375°F/Gas Mark 5 oven for about 20 minutes until black, stirring occasionally.

❋ Remove from the oven and chop well. Mix it with 225 ml (7 fl oz) of the water and then strain twice through muslin.

❋ Put both the flours in a large bowl and mix together. Stir in the remaining water and the sugar. Stir in the cup of black water mixture and strain again through muslin.

❋ Place the liquid in a stainless steel pan and slowly bring to a boil, stirring constantly, for about 20 minutes, until very thick—don't burn the bottom of the mixture.

❋ When thick, pour into ungreased shallow cake tins and leave to cool for 1 hour, then refrigerate for at least 1 hour, preferably overnight.

❋ To serve, warm the tins by dipping them in warm water and then inverting the mixture onto a plate. Cut the mixture into bite-sized pieces.

❋ Mix the coconut with the salt and sprinkle over the top.

IMITATION FRUIT

SERVES 6 TO 8

450 g (16 oz) dried mung beans

750 ml (1¼ pt) water

225 ml (7 fl oz) thin coconut milk

225 g (8 oz) sugar

edible food colourings

2 tbsp unflavoured powdered gelatin

This refined dessert was invented for the Thai royal court and originally was served only at the palace. Even today it is hardly common, because of the time and skill needed to fashion these perfect miniatures of fruits and vegetables. They are spectacular to serve to guests, but only attempt them on a day when you have plenty of time to spare!

❁ Place the mung beans in a container with the water and steam for about 15 minutes until soft. Pound them into a fine paste with a mortar and pestle or in a blender.

❁ Put the mung-bean paste in a pan with the coconut milk and 225 g (8 oz) of the sugar, and heat slowly, stirring constantly for about 15 minutes until very thick. Remove from the heat and set aside to cool.

❁ When cool, shape the paste into small fingertip-sized fruit and vegetable shapes—oranges, bananas—it's up to your imagination. Stick them on toothpicks and stand them in a styrofoam block.

❁ Using a small paint brush and food colourings in appropriate shades, paint the fruits.

❁ Heat 450 ml (¾ pt) of the water, 1 tablespoon of the sugar, and the gelatin in a pan until dissolved. Cool slightly and then dip in the painted fruits.

❁ Place them back on the foam and allow to dry for 15 minutes; then dip once more in the liquid, spinning the fruit slowly after removing them so that the syrup coats evenly.

❁ Leave to harden on the foam, then remove the toothpicks and decorate the fruits with any (non-poisonous) leaves of your choice, trimmed down to a small size.

JAPANESE
GREEN FRUIT SALAD

SERVES 6 TO 8	
6 tbsp unflavoured powdered gelatin	175 g (6 oz) green grapes, halved and seeded
450 ml (¾ pt) water	1 green apple, cored and sliced
150 ml (¼ pt) elderflower cordial	2 guavas
1 small melon, cut into balls	FOR THE SUGAR SYRUP
3 kiwi fruit, peeled and sliced	225 g (8 oz) granulated sugar
	375 ml (12 fl oz) water

Soak the gelatine in half the water for 15 minutes. Add the remaining water, place in a saucepan, and heat gently to dissolve. Leave to cool slightly before adding the elderflower cordial. Rinse a 18-cm (7-in) shallow square pan with water and pour in the gelatin mixture. Leave in a cold place to set.

❀ To make the syrup, put the sugar and water in a saucepan and heat until the sugar has dissolved. Boil rapidly for 2 to 3 minutes until slightly syrupy. Remove from the heat and cool.

❀ Place the melon in a large serving bowl. Add the kiwi fruit, grapes and apple.

❀ Add the cooled syrup. Peel the guavas, halve and scoop out the seeds. Slice and add to the salad.

❀ Quickly dip the pan with the set gelatin into hot water and turn out onto damp waxed paper. Cut into large cubes. Add to the salad just before serving.

STICKY RICE WITH MANGOES

SERVES 4 TO 6

450 g (16 oz) short-grain rice

3½ cups thin coconut milk

900 ml (1½ pt) sugar

½ tsp salt

½ tsp cornflour

2 ripe mangoes, peeled and sliced

A simple dessert (once you have mastered the steaming of sticky rice, see page 38), but always successful. It works because of contrasts: in flavour between the sweetness of the coconut milk and the yellow Thai mango, and in texture between the rice and the mango. Be sure to use the correct rice—this doesn't work with long-grain rice.

❀ Soak the rice in water for 4 hours, then rinse well 3 times in lukewarm water and drain very well.

❀ Line a strainer with muslin. Add the rice and place over a pan of boiling water—don't let the water touch the bottom of the rice. Cover and steam for about 30 minutes until fairly soft.

❀ Mix 750 ml (1¼ pt) of the coconut milk with the sugar and ¼ teaspoon of the salt. Stir in the rice and mix together well.

❀ Mix the remaining 150 ml (¼ pt) coconut milk with the ¼ teaspoon salt and cornflour in a small pan. Bring to a boil, then simmer for 2 minutes and cool.

❀ Place the sticky rice onto serving plates. Spoon the cornflour sauce over the top and arrange the mango slices around the edges.

INDEX

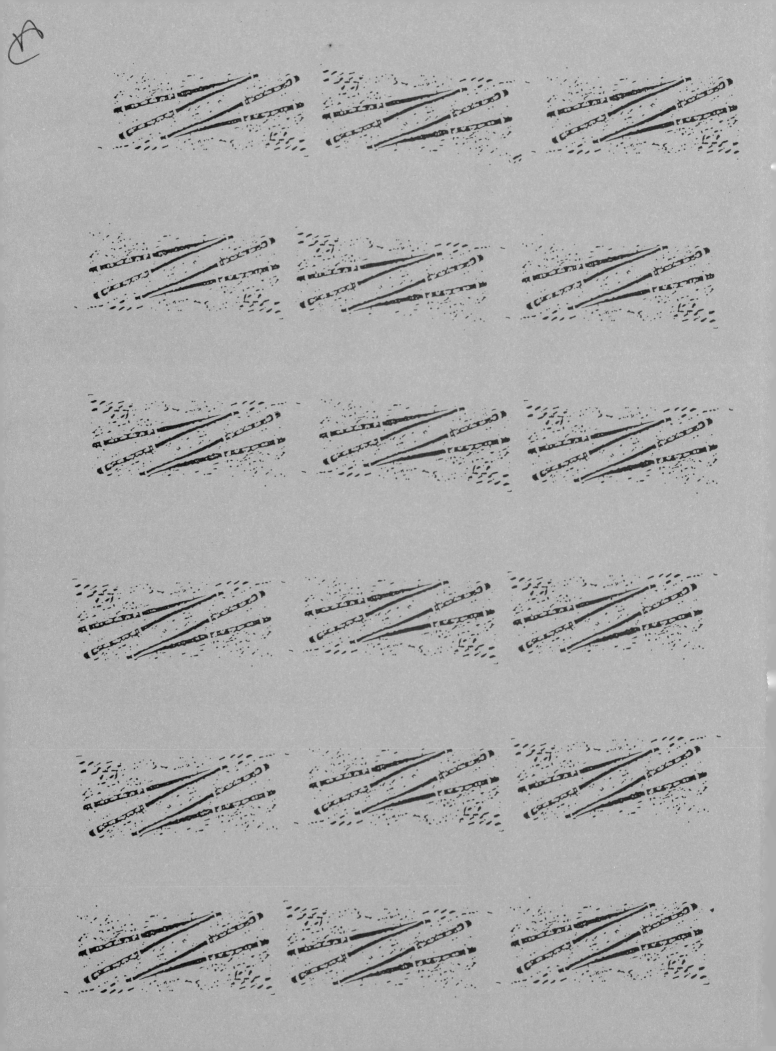